HEROINES OF HISTORY

Nikita Puri is an award-winning journalist who has spent over 12 years writing about people and places, science and environment, and arts and culture. She has worked with the India Today Group, *The Indian Express*, *Business Standard* and *Tech in Asia.*

Her understanding of India is shaped by a childhood marked by constant change, moving from city to city and discovering the country through local food, customs and languages. When she is not writing on the tech ecosystem spanning India and Southeast Asia, she is piecing together her next book, a work of fiction.

She currently lives in the city of magnificent rain trees, Bangalore. This is her first non-fiction book.

HEROINES OF HISTORY

Stories of India's Princesses

NIKITA PURI

RUPA

Published by
Rupa Publications India Pvt. Ltd 2023
7/16, Ansari Road, Daryaganj
New Delhi 110002

Sales centres:
Bengaluru Chennai
Hyderabad Jaipur Kathmandu
Kolkata Mumbai Prayagraj

P-ISBN: 978-93-5702-481-5
E-ISBN: 978-93-5702-486-0

First impression 2023

10 9 8 7 6 5 4 3 2 1

Printed in India

To my parents, who continue to believe
their daughters are capable of marvellous things,
my partner in all things dark and wonderful,
the friends who have promised to buy at
least one copy of this book
and the cats who've pretty much ruined my life.

CONTENTS

Introduction

My sister was born in Jhansi. I was too young at the time to remember much about the city, but I have flashes of memories that have survived the tides of time.

I especially remember the steep, downhill road right outside our house where I accidentally risked my sibling's life after standing on her pram and speeding downhill when no adult was around. I remember the busy market nearby where a cow ate the top of my vanilla soft serve with one swift move of the tongue, and no one believed me; and the time I was tricked into believing that Cadbury gems were 'seeds' that could sprout into a chocolate-bearing tree.

When we moved from Jhansi to Amritsar, I insisted on hanging around the horse-riding centre nearby. Too much of an overthinker to actually take any lessons, I was content feeding the five Australian-origin horses who rocked Indian names, like Trishul, who was a magnificent black stallion. This didn't mean that I didn't occasionally imagine myself riding the stallion with the wind in my hair.

As time passed, my visits to Trishul and his friends became rarer and rarer. But somehow, the image of a girl riding a horse never quite left me. It took me many years to register that even though I had left Jhansi behind, the dusty statue of Lakshmibai on her horse in that busy market—the one with the ice-cream-stealing cow—was a more significant part of my memories than I gave it credit for.

My family moved to many other cities after that, and I was privileged to have ample access to libraries almost everywhere we lived. However, across cities and times, there was a distinct lack of stories to which I could directly relate. I think this is why my early reading history is dotted with *Nancy Drew* books. This series about the young girl who worked as a detective had quite an impact on me. How else can I explain why, summer after summer, no matter where I was, I would look for clues to follow and cases to solve in places where there were neither clues nor cases worth an amateur detective's attention.

But Nancy Drew and I came from different worlds. I clung to her world as I could not find anything in my own that I could identify with. Make-believe adventures aside, hers was a white, American world. Mine was not.

Stories have immense power. Symbols also have immense power. When combined, they can fuel a child's imagination enough to make her look for adventures at every corner. They can even send her down a path where she seeks out story after story—be it hers or someone else's. As history has constantly proved, stories even hold the power to build up or overthrow governments.

But history is a strange beast. It has many ways of presenting itself to us and the perspective of each depends on the narrator and the ones who emerge victorious. In a world where there is a largely restrictive definition of what a 'victor' is, stories of remarkable women who did truly incredible things have gotten lost. This book is an attempt to revisit those stories.

This book started as an attempt to look into the lives of India's blue-blooded women. It ended with the realization that some of us continue to fight battles that were started long ago. The twenty-first century is still marked by surveys and reports about the percentage of women who have joined the professional workforce, how many startup founders and CEOs of multinational companies are women and so on. India's National Defence Academy was established in 1954, but the gates of this venerable academy finally opened to women only in 2021. These are just reflections of a world where women claiming their place next to their male counterparts is still newsworthy.

I wonder what Sophia—the daughter of Ranjit Singh, the Lion of Punjab—would say if she read the news today. Sophia risked everything so that women could get the right to vote and had a say in who their leaders would be. Noor, a descendant of Tipu Sultan, put herself right in the middle of a fascist stronghold as a spy during the Second World War. Raziya ruled over Delhi despite staunch opposition to the idea of a female leader.

Truth be told, there are no specific moulds that heroes and heroines fit into. For instance, while this book documents women taking on mighty challenges, like the time Velu Nachiyar led a rebellion to win her kingdom back, Gulbadan Begum's contributions to Indian history are of another kind altogether. A part of Emperor Akbar's family, Gulbadan Begum documented the lives of men and women during the Mughal era in a way that no historian of her time did.

Rajkumari Amrit Kaur, a passionate tennis player, found ways to use her position for good during India's freedom struggle. Another Indian royal, Rani Velu Nachiyar, raised an army comprising of men and women to win her kingdom back. This was at a time when all the kingdoms around hers were folding like a deck of cards against the might of the East India Company (EIC).

For the purpose of this book, I've taken certain moments—or rather, incidents—and retold them in ways I imagine they may have played out. These sections, where at times I have taken some creative liberty, are present in the beginning of each chapter. That said, I've tried my best to remain true to the story and the setting they were in.

All these stories wouldn't have been possible if not

for primary source research to draw from, like the works of Anita Anand, Shrabani Basu, Abraham Eraly, Archana Garodia Gupta and more.

We are surrounded by young minds who are growing up seeing statues of women like Lakshmibai and Velu Nachiyar, remarkable leaders who rode horses into battle. But reminders like these statues are far and few. For humans to grow and progress, it's crucial to know the lives of those who came before us.

This book is a documentation of the lives of some of India's princesses. Glimpses of the world these women lived in still exist today. These women didn't just inhabit the world, they also helped reshape it.

The stories in this book are their stories, but they are also our stories. Not only are their lives a part of our shared history, they can also serve as a catalyst when we need to make tough calls. Tales of overcoming hardships and going up against odds are timeless, after all.

Sophia

Worthier than Koh-i-noor

ENGLAND, 1914

The Royal Pavilion in Brighton, England, had been home to the royal families for decades. At the beginning of the First World War, it was converted into a military hospital.

Men born and raised on Indian soil sailed across seas to fight in the trenches of Belgium for this War. They were part of the British Indian Army. This was the first overseas journey many of them had ever made and it would also be the last for some of them. They were part of the Allied forces brought in to stop the advance of the Central powers.

They fought for weeks from mud-filled trenches to stop Germans on blood-soaked battlefields. They won this battle and marched into Paris to celebrate their victory. There, they were welcomed by cheering crowds on both sides of the streets. Some people even stepped forward to pin flowers on their uniforms.

Over a million Indian soldiers served in the First World War.[1] Over 70,000 of them died. No one could have known, back then, that over 12,000 Indian soldiers would pass through Brighton's hospitals.[2]

These soldiers were evacuated from the Western Front, a stretch of about 400 miles along France and Belgium. Yes, they had emerged as victors but they returned with a scarred legacy filled with loss and a deep longing for home. No amount of grand welcome parades could make them forget what they had witnessed on the frontline.

Far from the warmth of their home country, these soldiers were trying to rebuild themselves in a foreign land. Those who could do so, wrote letters to their families back home. Many of their families had no one who could understand these letters. They had to find a friend or a neighbour who could help them.

---

[1]'India and UK Commemorate Fallen Soldiers in World War 1', *Gov.UK*, 9 November 2018, https://tinyurl.com/3arym6sw. Accessed on 30 April 2023.

[2]Bacon, Kevin, 'Brighton's Role in Caring for Injured Indian First World War Soldiers', *Sussex Express*, 10 November 2021, https://tinyurl.com/yjr5njs8. Accessed on 30 April 2023.

The soldiers in Brighton had nine kitchens where they would make *chapati* to feed their fellow Indians. Many of these soldiers would sit out on the grounds of Brighton Pavilion. Turbaned and in uniform, with lathis in hand, they waited for their wounds to heal and fresh orders from their senior officers. Their dreary, slow-moving days were made somewhat better by strangers who volunteered to ensure the well-being of these soldiers. Among these strangers was a slight, well-dressed woman called Sophia.

As the horrors of the War continued to grow, more and more soldiers started coming into Brighton. Around this time, Sophia put aside her fine dresses and donned a nurse's uniform. She started devoting all her time and energy to nurse the wounded soldiers. She gave out signed photographs of herself and gave them ivory mirrors that boasted of fine craftsmanship. These mirrors would have cost a fortune in the soldiers' home country.

Sophia did not speak their language but the soldiers guessed that she had come from Indian ancestry. To most of the British, Sophia was a prominent socialite—a celebrity from Britain's upper crust. Like some others, she had been volunteering her time and energy towards Britain's War efforts.

This woman was the god-daughter of Queen Victoria, the monarch of Great Britain and the Empress of India. But she was more than that to the Indian soldiers, particularly to the Sikh ones who comprised nearly 20 per cent of the British Indian Army. She belonged to one of the most illustrious families of India. The Princess of Punjab, Sophia, was the daughter of a King without a kingdom.

Sophia's Story

If not for the diaries Sophia meticulously kept, and a few photographs and letters, her story could have been lost forever. But thanks to the works of scholars like Anita Anand and William Dalrymple, the stories of Sophia and her extended family have been made accessible to readers. Sophia's grandfather was Maharaja Ranjit Singh, a warrior-king whose empire once encompassed Khyber Pass in the west, Kashmir in the north, Tibet in the east and Sindh in the south. Punjab's empire flourished under him. Because of the battles he had won, Ranjit Singh was known as 'Sher-e-Punjab', or the 'Lion of Punjab'.

Among the Singh family's priceless royal treasures was the King's throne. Carved out of sheets of gold, the throne was crafted in the form of an opening lotus and was a reminder of a popular metaphor in Sikh scriptures that suggests that just like the lotus blooms unmindful of the murky waters around it, so must man remain untouched by worldly affairs. As the lotus that does not lose focus, so must one keep one's consciousness attuned to the Creator.

The Maharaja had a soft corner for gemstones: he loved diamonds and pearls. These he had in plenty, but there was something that had greater personal significance—the famed Koh-i-Noor, the world's most celebrated diamond. This stone's bloody history, among other reasons, made sure that it outshone the gold throne.

The Maharaja's life was marked by a series of conquests in which he won back lands that had been seized from India. When Nader Shah, the Emperor of Iran, invaded Delhi in 1739, he seized so much treasure from the Mughals that it took 700 elephants, 4,000 camels and 12,000 horses for him to take all the treasure.[3] The Koh-i-Noor diamond, which was till then on the Mughal Peacock Throne, was taken too. It was Ranjit Singh who brought this diamond back to India.[4] After numerous conquests, a series of strokes left Ranjit Singh bedridden and the King passed away in Lahore in 1839.

Much like his life, his funeral was a grand, astounding event. Soldiers carried his body to the pyre in a ship-shaped carriage that had sails made of silk and brocade. They

---

[3]Dalrymple, William, and Anita Anand, *Koh-i-noor: The Story of the World's Most Infamous Diamond*, Bloomsbury, 2017.

[4]Anand, Anita, *Sophia: Princess, Suffragette, Revolutionary*, Bloomsbury USA, 2016.

were preceded by melancholic musicians who announced the passage of the Maharaja's mortal remains. Four of his wives were also carried by soldiers in chairs as they sat dressed in their finest. A few of their female attendants also followed. These Queens and attendants would burn with the Maharaja, who was laid out on sandalwood.

A curious series of events followed his passing. The late Maharaja wanted to give the Koh-i-Noor to the Jagannath Temple in Odisha. However, after his passing, plans were made to pass it onto the British instead. The diamond (supposedly cursed) was hidden away as a fatal political drama played out.

At the end of this tumultuous drama, Punjab lost several maharajas and leaders of the State. One was poisoned with lead and mercury, another was shot. Another successor was supposedly battered to death. The only one left to take the throne of Punjab was Duleep Singh, the late Maharaja's youngest son. He was only five when he became the King. His mother, Maharani Jind Kaur (popularly known as Rani Jindan), came into prominence as his regent. But young Duleep Singh's reign was short-lived.

Thanks to a few treacherous men, the British walked into his court in Lahore victorious after the First Anglo-Sikh War of 1845–46. At that point, the British felt that they couldn't just remove the young King. He was a blood heir and his removal could incite a revolt, so instead they made him sign a treaty. The treaty said that they would part as friends and that he had to pay the British.[5]

Duleep Singh was too young to understand what was happening. The child had no say even when his mother was dragged out of the court and imprisoned because she refused to play by the rules of the British. For her defiance, Rani Jindan was sentenced to live out the rest of her days in a fortress far away from her son's court.

Rani Jindan, a bold and fearless woman, refused to be locked away in a fort. One day, she vanished from the fort. All the British found was a note she left behind. It read: 'For all your locks and your sentries, I got out by magic.'[6]

A sharp woman, Rani Jindan had enlisted the help of loyalists and friends to escape to Kathmandu. She had travelled across dressed as a pilgrim. As for the escape from the fort itself, according to oral stories, Rani Jindan had convinced a seamstress to trade clothes with her. The seamstress had pretended to be the Queen while Rani Jindan had walked past her captors with ease. She had tricked her guards into thinking she was a commoner and managed to flee her captors.

At that point, she did not know when she could see her son again.

After the Second Anglo-Sikh War of 1848–49, young Duleep Singh was officially removed from the throne.

---

[5]Dalrymple, William and Anita Anand, *Koh-i-noor: The Story of the World's Most Infamous Diamond*, Bloomsbury, 2017.
[6]Ibid.

But the British still feared that he could inspire a revolt, if given a chance. Owing to this his movements and meetings were put under strict watch. He could only meet other Indians under uncompromising supervision.

Using religion to divide and conquer people was a common tactic employed by the British. This tactic was used in Duleep Singh's case too. He had to convert to Christianity like some other Indian nobles. He was subsequently sent to England where he had to completely rebuild himself and try to forget the life he had left behind. Nicknamed the 'Black Prince of Perthshire', Duleep then grew up as an English prince. All connection with his past was severed.

Still, he managed to thrive under the affections of Queen Victoria and her Prince Consort. Both these royals were fond of the Lahore-born, turbaned king. They had even picked out a match for him. They hoped he'd marry Princess Victoria Gowramma (whose origins also lay in India). She was the daughter of Chikka Veera Rajendra, the last ruler of Kodagu (Coorg).

However, this match did not come to be. Duleep, whom Queen Victoria would refer to as her 'beautiful boy', married Bamba Müller instead. She was of German and Abyssinian ancestry and was raised by missionaries in Cairo. The couple had six children together. The Queen was so fond of Duleep's family that his eldest son, Victor, was christened twice since the Queen wasn't present at the first christening.

Sophia Alexandrovna Duleep Singh was Duleep Singh's fifth child. The Queen was fond of Sophia and readily became her godmother. Princess Sophia came into a world filled with the finest luxury imaginable. Her home, a property called Elveden Hall, stretched out on 17,000 acres. Duleep Singh had left India, but the style of things that once marked his father's courts had journeyed with him to England. That's why Sophia's early days were spent playing on an estate that was fitted out in the Rajput style. The English home resembled a Mughal palace with its marble floors and decorative mirrors.

Duleep Singh kept cheetahs, baboons, leopards, hawks, ducks, parrots and many more animals to add to the magnificence of this home. Many of these animals, purely serving as decorative additions, weren't meant to survive the brutal winter of Britain. Much like how his birds found their lives slipping away every winter, so did Duleep Singh's wealth. The opulent and extravagant life he had grown accustomed to started disappearing. His was a life of exorbitant excesses, destined to run out sooner or later.

When the lures of youth and wealth began to fade, it's likely that Duleep Singh began to wonder how much he had lost. Separated from his mother and his people, he was dependent solely on what the Crown gave him. It's very likely that if things had gone another way, he could have had a kingdom of his own. In an attempt to claim his birthright, Duleep (along with his wife and six children) tried to move back to Punjab. They were stopped at the port of Aden, Yemen, and were unceremoniously turned away. They were told they would be arrested if they didn't go back to Britain. Sophia was only 10 at the time of this incident. Her family was displaced and mistreated and things were about to get much worse.

Her father was against the idea, but her mother brought the family back to London. The India Office sent some amount of pension for the family, as was customary. But those allowances were never enough to pacify Duleep Singh. The money allotted to take care of their needs was not enough to keep them together either.

Still enraged with the British Empire, Duleep Singh is said to have left his family and moved away. He managed to meet his mother and even re-converted to Sikhism, the faith of his forefathers. But, most likely, the feeling of being cheated consumed him. After he left, Sophia and her siblings had to watch their mother give in to despair and alcoholism. Their family was still the talk of the town, as it always had been, but now their downfall was the source of gossip.

As mentioned in *Sophia: Princess, Suffragette, Revolutionary*, it was at this juncture that Queen Victoria intervened to ensure Sophia's family had a place to stay. They moved from Sophia's birth home, Elveden Hall in Suffolk, to Faraway House at the Hampton Court Palace. This was a 'grace and favour' residence—it belonged to the monarch but Sophia was allowed to stay there rent-free under the Queen's guardianship.

Though all their material needs were taken care of, the family continued to have a hard time. Alienated from her husband, Sophia's mother passed away. One of her brothers, Edward, also passed away. He was the youngest among Sophia's siblings, and his death hit her hard.

Her estranged father was living in Paris at that time. He was trying to organize a revolt against the British in India. Duleep Singh had also remarried and had other children. Sophia was 17 when she heard that her father was no more—he had died alone and in poverty in a hotel room in Paris.[7]

Many believed that Sophia, a quiet girl, would give in to grief in light of these tragedies, but she emerged stronger from her trials. Sophia was well-educated. She had studied chemistry at Cambridge University but her first and foremost role, like other women born into high British society, was to be a socialite. And the Princess had excelled in that role. She would regularly be the toast of society columns.

A fashion icon often seen in the latest of European designs, Sophia also had a great collection of dogs. She had French Poodles and other toy dog breeds that she would take for walks in the royal gardens. She was also

---

[7]'"Black Prince" Rekindles Debate on Duleep Singh's Last Rites', *The Tribune*, 23 July 2017, https://tinyurl.com/59pwf8wy. Accessed on 23 June 2023.

an expert horse rider and a competitive hockey player.[8] Newspaper columns also described her as a 'first-rate cyclist'.[9]

Sophia and her siblings, by virtue of their birth and family status, had front-row seats to the affairs of the British court. They were anglicized aristocrats and their education and upbringing resembled the one their father had.

When they came of age, Sophia and her sisters (Bamba and Catherine) made their debut in the British court in May 1885. They were dressed in exquisite white gowns, fine pearls and lace veils for this event. This was a big day. It was their formal introduction to English society—an induction of sorts.

England had given them a lot but it wasn't enough. The three Singh sisters longed to see India—the country their father had deeply longed to return to when he was alive. When the Delhi Durbar of 1903 was announced, the Singh sisters saw it as an opportunity to visit the shores of their ancestors.

The Durbar was an exceedingly grand spectacle meant to mark the coronation of Edward VII, Queen Victoria's eldest son, and his wife Queen Alexandra as

---

[8]Anand, Anita, *Sophia: Princess, Suffragette, Revolutionary*, Bloomsbury USA, 2016.

[9]Roy, Nilanjana S., 'Speaking Volumes: India's Suffragette-Princess', *nilanjanaroy.com*, 16 February 2015, https://tinyurl.com/5f9kr66k. Accessed on 23 June 2023.

the Emperor and Empress of India. According to Anita Anand, at one point, Edward VII was among Sophia's father's closest friends. Dulcep Singh would regularly invite Edward VII to his estate. The two would go out on grand hunting parties together.

When Sophia's eldest brother Victor married Anne Coventry, the daughter of the ninth Earl of Coventry, the union kicked up a storm. This was the first time that an Indian prince had married an English noblewoman. It was only due to Edward VII's support that things remained under control.

Affairs of the Crown were sometimes nasty. Here was Edward VII, being crowned as the Emperor of India—a land, a part of which the Singh family once had a stronghold on. All the sisters wanted was to visit the country of their forefathers and witness their father's friend being crowned. But when they expressed their desire to travel to India, their request was denied.

Like in their father's case, the British felt that the presence of the Singh sisters could kindle a rebellion. They were, after all, symbolic of the lost Sikh Empire. Even though they were not invited, the Singh sisters still went ahead and boarded a ship to India.

And it was there, in the land of her forefathers, that Sophia found herself facing racism for the first time. Officers of the EIC treated her like they treated other brown-skinned Indians, as second-class citizens in their own country. While the sisters all saw the same things, it affected them differently. The coronation was designed to showcase the pomp and power of the British Empire. But the racism that Sophia experienced was a thoroughly shocking backdrop for one of the greatest celebrations in the world.

The officers of the EIC—men who came from the land she was born in and had identified with for so long—completely shunned and mistreated her. In stark contrast, the Sikhs, with whom she had never had any contact, welcomed her with open arms. This was despite her not knowing their language or customs.

All of this was an eye-opener for someone like her, who had previously only known the privilege and protection her high-born status gave her. This experience changed Sophia forever, making her painfully aware of the bubble she had been in as the Queen's god-daughter.

Perhaps the young woman thought this was her only chance to see India. Perhaps she hoped to return again. We shall never know... But while she was in India, she grabbed the opportunity to travel across the country. From Lahore to the rest of undivided India, Sophia saw poverty and famine everywhere she went. She also saw how the British mistreated the people of India.

Those who recognized the Princess as Ranjit Singh's granddaughter in Lahore reminded her of her family's heritage and reputation. She was in a land where the streets were alive with tales of how her grandfather had consolidated the Sikh Empire; how he had kept the

Afghans out; and how he first went to battle when he was only 10.

As mentioned in the book *Sophia: Princess, Suffragette, Revolutionary* by Anita Anand, all of Sophia's riches and comfort paled in comparison when she realized what her family had been forced to leave. No amount of wealth compared to what she felt when walked the lands of her father's birth nation. It was like she had found a missing piece of herself—a piece of a puzzle she didn't even know she was missing.

Knowing where you come from has immense power; it can change you. As Sophia came to terms with her family's legacy, she noticed that the nationalist leaders were gaining popularity. Across India, the call to rise up against the British was gaining momentum.

The British were right in their precaution to keep Sophia's family from returning. Now that they were in India, their loyalties towards the Empire were fading.

The easiest way to write a new history is to erase the old one. Disconnect enough people from their roots and culture and half the battle is won. The British had perfected this tool—to divide and rule—and it almost never failed them. Disconnecting the Singh family from their roots was also in line with this plan. In the case of the Singh sisters, though, it didn't go as well as planned.

Filled with a newfound sense of belonging, Sophia spent more and more time in the company of Indian freedom fighters. Even after she returned home, she continued to exchange letters with Indian revolutionaries like Gopal Krishna Gokhale, Sarla Devi and Lala Lajpat Rai. Sophia looked up to Rai in particular.

After Sophia left India, she learnt that Rai had been charged with sedition. This act, in some ways, was a tipping point for the young woman. It cemented in her a hatred for the officials of the British Empire who had wronged her people. 'Oh, you wicked English, how I long for your downfall. How I loathe you all,' she wrote in her diary.[10]

Sophia's friends, back in Britain, probably expected her to return with tales of great riches and exotic delights from her visit to India. All these minor royals in the British court had expected Sophia to join their bridge clubs and crochet circles, but they were in for a surprise.

By the time Sophia returned to the shores of England in 1909, she was a changed person. She had seen the world for how it truly was and nothing could make her turn away from life's harsher realities.

Mulling over all that she had seen and learnt in India, Sophia could no longer go back to the life of excess she lived before. She needed to do more than just breed prized dogs and promulgate fashion trends. It was during this time of introspection that Sophia also must have realized Britain's shoddy treatment of lascars.

---

[10]Anand, Anita, *Sophia: Princess, Suffragette, Revolutionary*, Bloomsbury USA, 2016.

The lascars were Indian seamen—a majority of them from Bengal and Punjab (in undivided India) and some from parts of modern-day Pakistan. When ships laden with spices and supplies left India for Britain, they were often in need of men to work on the ships. The men who had come with them from Britain would either be dead or would look for employment elsewhere. Hence, there was a need for fresh manpower. In fact, by the early 1900s, the empire of Great Britain and the EIC had become extremely dependent on India for manpower.

Once they reached Britain, these lascars were left to fend for themselves. They had to wait for weeks, sometimes months, before they could find employment on another ship headed towards India.

While they lived in London, waiting for a chance to see their families again, many were treated miserably by their British employers. Some of these seamen were physically tortured; some were even forced to eat meat forbidden by their religious beliefs; and some lived as slaves in the hovels of London.

Stuck in a strange place, these men had shocking stories of what they had experienced. The horrible scenes and accounts she saw and heard caused Sophia to become actively involved in the betterment of their lives. She put in the effort and used her access to high society to raise funds and create a safe house for these men—a place where they could be fed and sheltered.

Besides working for the welfare of these men, Sophia

continued her campaigns for the release of Lala Lajpat Rai. This course of social activism led her to find kindred spirits and like-minded people, who believed in the principles of equality and justice and fought for them.

∽

The turn of the twentieth century was a crucial point in Britain's history as the cause of women's suffrage was gaining great momentum. Suffrage—the right to vote—was something that women in those times did not have, and Sophia easily became an ally of the movement. In fact, much of Sophia's life is known to the world only because of her reputation as a prominent suffragette.

In April 1913, a picture in the *Daily Mail* created something of a scandal in the British court.[11] The picture was of Sophia. She had been photographed standing with a large satchel swung across her fur coat holding up copies of the newspaper, *The Suffragette.* Right next to her was a placard that read 'Suffragette Revolution'. 'Votes for Women,' she would shout while standing outside the Hampton Court Palace and her own place of residence.[12]

To see the Queen's god-daughter selling newspapers on the street was utterly shocking for British sensibilities.

---

[11]Ibid.

[12]'Sophia Duleep Singh: The Indian Princess Who Fought for Women's Rights', *Historic Royal Palaces,* https://tinyurl.com/33fwnhrt. Accessed on 23 June 2023.

But this was Sophia's way of drawing attention to a cause she strongly believed in. She knew well enough that her background would help publicize the cause, but it was not safe for her to take a political stand. After all, one of Sophia's mentors, prominent political activist Emmeline Pankhurst, had just been sentenced to three years of imprisonment with hard labour. Emmeline's crime was leading suffragette activities and fighting for women's right to vote.

Sophia could easily connect with this movement. Her father and sister (Bamba) had spent much of their adult life in the quest of an impossible dream. And no matter how much they wanted to claim their rightful place in history, the world had changed too much for that to happen. When his people last saw him, Duleep Singh was a young boy who signed away his throne and gave one of the largest cut diamonds in the world—the Koh-i-Noor—to the British.

Instead of grappling for a lost cause, Sophia must have realized that she had to choose her battles. She saw how the women around her were fighting for equal rights. In them was the same fire that she had seen burning in the hearts of those fighting for India's freedom. In their cause, Sophia found a reason worthy enough to go to battle. She saw the similarities between how women in Britain and Indians in India were denied a say in how their government functioned. These became overlapping concerns for her.

Sophia, a radical firebrand, joined a highly political organization—the Women's Social and Political Union. She also became friends with activists such as Una Dugdale and the Pankhurst sisters—the other leaders of the Suffragette movement alongside Emmeline Pankhurst.

Over 300 women marched to the British Parliament on 18 November 1910. The march was to garner support for the suffragette cause but it was halted when cops came out in large numbers. What followed was excessive police brutality, with many of the women being assaulted. Sophia had marched with them. Her name appears among the hundreds who were arrested on that fateful day. The date has gone down in history as 'Black Friday'. Sophia is remembered as one of the youngest leaders of the movement. Her fighting spirit echoed the strength of her ancestors.

During the march, when Sophia saw a policeman hitting a woman, she physically put herself between them. The policeman recognized Sophia. He fled the scene but Sophia made note of his badge number. She complained to the authorities about him. Her complaints climbed up all the way to Winston Churchill, the then home secretary of Britain. Churchill, who once referred to Gandhi as 'a half-naked fakir',[13] was a crafty man and he gave his staff explicit instructions to ignore Sophia.

---

[13]James, Robert Rhodes (ed.), *Winston S. Churchill: His Complete Speeches, 1897–1963: 1908–1913*, Chelsea House Publishers, New York, 1974.

However, she was not one to be ignored. In 1911, she waited outside 10 Downing Street for Prime Minister Herbert Asquith. As he appeared in his car, she flung herself in front of the moving vehicle. One can only imagine his shock to see someone suddenly appear in front of his car. Determined to not be ignored this time, Sophia thrust a poster forward that read 'Votes for Women'.

Sophia's acts of defiance against the government continued in many ways. When there was a census survey, for instance, some had a straightforward reason for not wanting to participate in it. The thinking was that if they wouldn't be treated as citizens whose voice was equal to that of men, why should they be counted as citizens at all?

This line of thinking seemed extreme to the lawmakers. They even allotted police officers in plainclothes to monitor movements of people around a few houses in London, which they thought housed people with these pro-women's rights beliefs.[14] The officers stood there all night long, from 10.00 p.m. to 6.00 a.m., just keeping watch and making notes.

Like many others silently supporting the Suffragette Movement, Sophia could have chosen not to actively participate in it. But passive protest was not in this firebrand's nature. Not only did she boycott the survey, she

---

[14]Iglikowski-Broad, Vicky, '"No Vote, No Census": The 1911 Suffrage Census Protests', *The National Archives*, 2 April 2020, https://tinyurl.com/yevxtcyk. Accessed on 30 April 2023.

also defaced the census document. 'No Vote, No Census. As women do not count, they refuse to be counted,' she scrawled across the form.[15]

In 1838, Queen Victoria opened the Hampton Palace so that the public could enjoy its architecture and splendid art collection. It attracted millions of people. When the suffragette movement started seeing traction, for the first time in 70 years those galleries were closed. The government feared that the suffragettes would undertake violent means to voice their protest. It would have been splendid for the movement for equal rights to have a champion as noteworthy as the Queen's god-daughter.

On 30 December 1913, the *Daily Mail* published a picture of Sophia wrapped up in fine black furs and wearing an elaborate feather hat.[16] She wasn't leaving a social gathering but the police court in Feltham. She had been arrested before but this was the first time she was facing prosecution. The charge against Sophia—who had become involved with the Tax Resistance League and wore a medal and pin announcing the same—was unpaid taxes for her dogs, carriage and the help.

Sophia had already been fined twice for not paying taxes. She turned up in court with all the grace expected of a woman of her social standing.

---

[15]Ibid.

[16]Anand, Anita, *Sophia: Princess, Suffragette, Revolutionary*, Bloomsbury USA, 2016.

In court, Sophia's lawyer, Leon Castello informed the jury that his client would speak for herself. She did and what a scandal it created! Her speech was splashed across almost all newspapers. It read:

> I am unable conscientiously to pay money to the state, as I am not allowed to exercise any control over its expenditure, neither am I allowed any voice in the choosing of members of Parliament, whose salaries I have to help to pay. This is very unjustified. When the women of England are enfranchised and the State acknowledges me as a citizen, I shall, of course, pay my share willingly towards its upkeep, if I am not a fit person for the purposes of representation, why should I be a fit person for taxation?[17]

Sophia still had friends in high places. Every time the government tried to auction off her belongings for unpaid taxes, her friends would buy them back. It's likely that Sophia understood her societal status afforded her great privilege and security. But she seemed willing to push the boundaries of this security and risk it all.

Officers of the British court had always kept a close eye on members of the Singh family, especially after Duleep Singh had moved to Paris. They had kept his children under watch even after his passing. His eldest,

---

[17]Ibid.

Victor, had become a British Army officer. The second-born, Frederick, was a staunch monarchist and was loyal to the British Crown. Sophia's sister Catherine was also involved with the suffrage campaign but after spending some time in England, Catherine moved away to Germany to start a new life and even helped a Jewish family flee Nazi Germany and settle in England. However, their sister Bamba had always felt India's pull quite strongly. She moved to Lahore. When borders were drawn up between India and Pakistan, she was furious as those demarcations split Punjab into two halves. With siblings like hers, the British could not have known that it was Sophia that they had to watch out for.[18]

When the First World War was announced, Sophia joined a protest march of 10,000 women for not allowing women to be a part of the war effort.[19] When wounded soldiers started filling up Britain's hospitals, Sophia paused her suffragette work and turned her attention to helping those soldiers.

She became a member of the Voluntary Aid Detachment (VAD), a unit of the Red Cross. This was a section of civilians who cared for soldiers evacuated from battle. Sophia was also involved with the Soldier's

---

[18]'Gallery Named after Duleep Singh to Come Up at UK Museum', *The Tribune*, 19 July 2015, https://tinyurl.com/mv8bxptv. Accessed on 23 June 2023.

[19]Anand, Anita, *Sophia: Princess, Suffragette, Revolutionary*, Bloomsbury USA, 2016.

Welfare Fund. She devoted a significant amount of her time to raise funds for Indian soldiers fighting as part of the British Indian Army. They had been posted all over—from the trenches of Belgium to the riverbanks of Tigris and Euphrates in Mesopotamia.

From warm clothes and sturdy shoes to chocolates and cigarettes, Sophia arranged whatever she could for the soldiers. She even organized 'Flag Days' to raise money for those wounded in the War, the first of which was on 19 October 1916. British and Indian women came together on these days to sell flags decorated with elephants and stars. Sophia also entertained Indian soldiers who were part of a peace contingent at her home in Hampton Court in September 1919.[20]

After the First World War finally came to an end, Sophia was invited to join the select group of women who comprised the Suffragette Fellowship. This was a great honour and recognized her contribution for the cause. By the Second World War, Sophia had left her Hampton home to move to a village called Penn in Buckinghamshire, into a bungalow named 'Rathenrae'.

This time, the war was much closer to home. Germany sent planes to drop bombs on Britain's cities. Whenever an enemy plane was sighted, loud sirens pierced the air. People were instructed to turn off their lights, shrouding

---

[20]'Sophia Duleep Singh', *Making Britain,* https://tinyurl.com/y3drbz67. Accessed on 23 June 2023.

entire cities in darkness to ensure these planes didn't find a target to hit.

To further avoid casualties during these bombings, children were separated from their parents and sent away from London. They were handed over to those in the countryside to wait out the War. Sophia took in three children to save them from the bombing that went on for 11 weeks.

∽

Sophia, a woman caught in between different worlds, never married. Instead, she became a godmother to her housekeeper Bosie's daughter, Drovna. According to Anita Anand's book, she would tell Drovna about how women like her had marched and fought tooth and nail for women's rights.

It is very possible that if not for the diaries Sophia meticulously kept—and a few photographs and letters—her story could have been lost forever. This would have been a real shame considering how Sophia and her family's story is a significant chapter in the intricately linked histories of India and Britain. No one could have predicted that the shy Sophia, who grew up in favour of the British court, would one day become a formidable revolutionary. It took only one visit to India to shape Sophia into the person she was meant to be.

In 1918, the British Parliament passed the Representation

of the People Act, which gave women the right to vote. In 2018, when the British government marked the centenary of this law, a stamp was issued in Sophia's honour. The once-controversial photo of Sophia selling *The Suffragette* outside the Hampton Court Palace is now on this stamp.[21]

India is yet to recognize the many ways in which Sophia, a life-long warrior like her ancestors, battled for the cause of human rights. She passed away in 1948 at the age of 72 in Buckinghamshire. Sophia was cremated in accordance with Sikh rites, as per her wishes.

Despite spending almost all her life in Britain and having much of her family buried there, Sophia wanted her ashes to be brought to India and scattered there. Her father had also wished for the same but his wishes were never granted.

Sophia's wishes were honoured. The Princess of Punjab was finally home. She became one with the land of her forefathers. In May 2023, Sophia's contribution was formally recognized when the UK installed a blue plaque in front of her residence. (Buildings of historical importance are marked by blue plaques in the UK.) If her family had continued to hold on to her grandfather's legacy, Sophia could have been one of the few caretakers of the precious Koh-i-Noor.

---

[21]'Indian Princess Sophia Alexandra Duleep Singh Gets UK's Royal Mail Stamp', *ZeeNews*, 7 February 2018, https://tinyurl.com/cthp729j. Accessed on 23 June 2023.

Every time India and England talk of that diamond, dear reader, think of what Sophia did for the two nations. And every time the question of nationality comes up, dear reader, think about Sophia—who was born and raised elsewhere but found a calling in both India and Britain as a way to navigate different identities.

Gulbadan

An Unconventional Witness

SURAT, 1575

There was a hustle-bustle in the town. The horses that had just come into town had elaborate saddles, which signified that they belonged to the royal court. The horses and their riders pulled up at the destined spot and waited for their host to receive them. They were confident of being well-received, as the man they represented was no ordinary citizen. They were envoys of Akbar, the King who later became the most well-known Mughal emperor in India's incredibly rich history.

The host, Gulbadan Begum, welcomed the riders who had journeyed on dusty paths leading up to Surat. This was not her permanent home, just a house she was living in temporarily. The most prominent in this group of visitors was Prince Murad, Akbar's son.

For many moons, the Princess had been preparing for an ambitious journey. So, in many ways, it was also a trip she had never made before. Gulbadan, and a few other women from the Mughal court, were planning to sail from the port of Surat and go on a pilgrimage to the holy shrine of Mecca (in modern-day Saudi Arabia).

This was a voyage that Gulbadan Begum had longed to take. After a long period of trouble and uncertainty, there was a semblance of peace and stability on the sea route that she needed to take. Though Emperor Akbar had proclaimed his dominion over much of India, the seas beyond the port of Gujarat were a different ball game altogether. Here, it was the Portuguese who had mastery over the trade and pilgrimage routes. They were known to resort to systematic piracy when they fancied it.

After being stuck at Surat for close to a year, Gulbadan Begum finally paid a hefty bribe so that she could leave the port safely. And she didn't pay in coins or gold; the Begum's bribe came in the form of the entire city of Bulsar (modern-day Valsad).

Prince Murad had turned up at the Begum's residence, as he had been directed by his father to act as her guide and accompany her convoy. As a woman of great standing in the *durbars* of the Mughal court, Gulbadan Begum bore no ill will or grouse against Prince Murad but she refused to have him travel with her. She knew well enough what the prince represented. He was barely six but customs dictated that the prince was senior enough to guide people far older than him.

Gulbadan Begum wasn't one to easily fall in line and do what was expected of her. She was the daughter of Babur, the first monarch of the Mughal Empire in India. Much of this story is pieced together from the chronicles she put together herself.

GULBADAN'S STORY

The year 1523 was a time of celebration for Zahir ud-Din Muhammad, better known to the world as Babur, who had been a lord in Kabul for close to two decades. A child had just been born to him. Since her Persian name, Gulbadan, translates to 'with a body like the rose', Western historians like Rumer Godden call her Princess Rosebody. Most of the information about the Princess comes to us from a translation of the *Humayun Nama*, which was written by Gulbadan herself.

Babur belonged to one of the largest dynasties that India would ever see—the Mughals. Babur's oldest son,

Humayun, was his successor. Gulbadan Begum was Humayun's half-sister.

Gulbadan was brought up mainly by Maham Begum, the chief of Babur's wives, although her birth mother was Dildar Begum. English historian Rumer Godden, while comparing Babur and Henry VIII, has said that if Gulbadan was born in London instead of Kabul, Henry VIII would have been her father's equivalent. According to her, Henry VIII 'was given the title Defender of the Faith, just as her father, the Emperor Babur, would become Ghazi, Avenger of God'.[1]

Gulbadan was barely two when Babur set out to cross the Khyber Pass with a small army and challenge Ibrahim Lodi (of the Afghan Lodi dynasty). He won this battle in 1526. History remembers this as the Battle of Panipat, and the victory gave Babur a strong foothold in India. This was one of the first battles where gunpowder and field artillery brought by the Mughals was extensively used.[2]

Even as he started anew, Babur yearned for the land of his ancestors. Such was his love for his homeland that one time in his camp in Agra, Babur burst into tears when he spotted melons from Kabul.[3] This was Gulbadan

---

[1]Godden, Rumer, *Gulbadan: Portrait of a Rose Princess at the Mughal Court*, India Research Press, 2007.

[2]Dixit, Rekha, 'Big Guns Arrive', *The Week*, https://tinyurl.com/2p8accpx. Accessed on 23 June 2023.

[3]Begam, Gulbadan, *The Humayun Nama*, Annette S. Beveridge (trans.), Royal Asiatic Society, 1902.

Begum's lineage—people who respected their past while embracing the present with open arms.

Babur wrote in his memoirs about a deal with Rana Sanga, a Rajput King. Rana had previously offered to support Babur against the Lodi dynasty.[4] But the Rana's forces never turned up, neither did any messenger. Babur accused Rana Sanga of breaching their agreement. This lead to the Battle of Khanwa (1527) in Rajasthan. Babur won this war too.

These two victories secured his hold over a land he hoped to make his own. His family, which lived in Kabul, joined him in Agra, their new home.

Along with Maham Begum, Gulbadan made the journey with her father across the Indus River. She was six at that time. When she saw her father, she fell at his feet. Babur welcomed the child with great affection, seating her on his knee. He asked her about her journey and general well-being. She took every opportunity to stay near her father, now that they were united again. If he travelled somewhere, she accompanied him on horseback.

However, her time with her father was short-lived as Babur fell ill soon after. Fearing that he may never recover, Babur found suitable matches for Gulbadan's older sisters. Both their names started with 'Gul' as well (Gulrang and Gulchehra). He then addressed his officers; counselled Humayun; and formally declared him as his

---

[4]Ibid.

successor. 'Do nothing to your brothers even though they may deserve it,' Babur advised Humayun. Reflecting on this incident, Gulbadan has written thus: 'At these words hearers and onlookers wept and lamented. His own blessed eyes were also filled with tears.' [5]

Babur passed away on 26 December 1530. He was in India for only four years and could not have foreseen the influence and power his descendants would go on to wield. Gulbadan recalled the event of his death in these words: 'Black fell the day. We passed that ill-fated day each in a hidden corner.'[6] According to the *Baburnama*, Babur's body was taken back to Kabul and was laid to rest in a place he had chosen for himself long ago.

Humayun became the emperor after that. History remembers his name well enough, but the stories of those around him (like Gulbadan) have faded with time.

What we do know about Gulbadan is that she was well-educated. She excelled in calligraphy and had a personal library of books, collected from various places. Unfortunately, there is no substantial account of her own life. She was witness to a lot. She saw how her brother lost the empire their father had founded, and then attempted to reclaim it bit by bit. She also saw how Akbar took this empire forward.

The story of the Mughal Empire has been told many times by many people. But each narration brings its

---

[5]Ibid.

[6]Ibid.

own perspectives, and this is where Gulbadan's insights come in. For instance, Gulbadan's writings are meant to be records from an insiders' perspective—who better to document stories about lives in the Mughal *zenana* than someone who lived there herself.

As feminist historians have pointed out, there's no dearth of source material when it comes to writing the histories of men. However, the documentation of women's stories has been so sparse that historical women are almost invisible. Like the first coat of watercolour on a canvas, women's stories are pushed behind. They are only kept to strengthen the mainstream stories.

Even when Gulbadan wrote her account of the time—a diary of sorts—she wrote very little about herself. Instead, she wrote about her family and the court. She was mostly kind to her brother (Hindal) in her writings, despite him rebelling against Humayun. She wrote of things that the scholars of her time ignored—small incidents that can change how we look at the Mughals. She also wrote of war and survival.

In 1540, Humayun and his forces were fighting Sher Shah Suri—the Sultan of the Suri Empire and the man who had won Hindal's loyalty. As it was customary for the Mughals to travel with their families everywhere, even the women followed them to battle areas. During this battle, Humayun's horse slipped and drowned in the river. The Emperor himself was almost carried away by water currents but was saved by a water-carrier named Nizam.

Presumably, it was while narrating the account of this battle that Humayun spoke to Gulbadan about his daughter who had gone missing—Aqiqa Begum. Humayun's next remarks, recorded by Gulbadan, are the closest we get to learning about Gulbadan's own marriage. Gulbadan has written that Humayun said that he almost didn't recognize her at first because when he had gone away to prepare for battle, she used to wear the *taq* and now wore the *lachak*. The taq, according to Beveridge, is a cap worn by unmarried Mughal women, and the lachak referred to a scarf on the head (in a particular fashion), which was worn by married women. She was married to a nobleman from Genghis Khan's family called Khizr Khwaja Khan when she was 17. She has written very little about her husband.

After Humayun lost to Sher Shah at the Battle of Kannauj in 1540, he was forced to go into exile. This marked a temporary end to the Mughal rule in India. His extended family, staying true to a lifetime of constant wandering, had to leave for Kabul. When Humayun returned to reclaim Agra, Gulbadan Begum did not accompany him.

On 24 January 1556, when the *azaan* was heard, Humayun was descending the stairs from the library. His arms were full of books. As was his habit, he bowed in reverence when he heard the prayer summon and fell down the stairs in a freak accident. He died three days later. Far away from her brother's deathbed, Gulbadan did not make the journey to see him one last time.[7] Humayun's son, Akbar, brought Gulbadan back to Agra after his father passed away.

Two years after her brother's death, Gulbadan Begum joined Akbar's imperial household in Agra. It was only with Akbar establishing a base in Agra that the Mughals regained a foothold in India. It was here that the zenana was established, which flummoxed outsiders, who had no idea about it. It was a place not just for Akbar's wives but also for his mother, aunts and the women in his extended family.

Akbar's mother, Hamida Banu Begum, also had a library in the zenana. She was also known to have a special copy of an illustrated version of the Ramayana.[8]

Both mother and son had great affection for Gulbadan. Akbar would insist on having his aunt's tent near his own whenever they travelled together. This was a mark of respect from the Emperor—only those closest to him could set up accommodation near his place of dwelling.

Gulbadan spent much of her adult life in Agra and Fatehpur Sikri, except for seven fascinating years when she led a team of women on a voyage that was nothing short of dangerous. This voyage, as mentioned earlier,

---

[7]Eraly, Abraham, *Emperors of the Peacock Throne: The Saga of the Great Mughals*, Penguin India, 2007.

[8]Seyller, John William, Marika Sardar and Audrey Truschke, 'Queen Mother of Mughal India', *Museum of Islamic Art*, 2020.

was across pirate-infested waters—from the port of Surat to the holy city of Mecca.

She set out for Mecca in 1575. And what a long journey that was, considering that it took seven years for her to return to the safety of Akbar's court.

No matter how many times Akbar insisted that she be accompanied by men of high rank, Gulbadan declined the offer. Akbar agreed to hold back the Prince and for Gulbadan to travel with the women she had banded together.

At that time, trips, even a pilgrimage, to certain countries in West Asia (Middle East) required women to have suitable male escorts when they travelled. Considering this, Gulbadan Begum not only set forth on a challenging journey (in a time very different from ours) but also stood her ground against Akbar.

She had grown old by the time she went to Mecca. She had seen the rise and fall of Babur and her brother Humayun, and the beginning of Akbar's reign. She had seen India's society changing and transforming, up close. She had also witnessed how international politics had begun to play out in the land where she had grown up.

But neither her advanced age nor the society's expectations could keep the Begum from doing what she wanted to—even if it meant sailing on unpredictable, tumultuous waters.

According to historian Ruby Lal, Gulbadan stayed in Arabia for three-and-a-half years. Two ships sent to pick Gulbadan and her band of women were wrecked midway, leaving the party stranded at the port of Aden.

To top that, despite being aware of their royal lineage, the Turkish governor was discourteous to his guests. Akbar was in Kabul, far from his capital, and it's likely that he couldn't send help immediately. Most historians estimate they were stuck at Aden for almost a year.

One can only wonder how long it took Gulbadan and her troupe to get their sea legs. It makes one wonder if they got tired of the endless view of the same horizon that greeted them, day after day, on the trip to Mecca and back. One wonders if they longed for the sights and sounds of home, like Gulbadan's father once had. But Gulbadan never wrote of these things, and her adventures and experiences of this time are left to our imagination alone. The few details we have of Gulbadan's own journey to Mecca are from Abu'l-Fazl ibn Mubarak's *Akbarnama.*

After braving great stormy winds, inhospitable terrains and disrespectful hosts, Gulbadan finally touched Indian shores. Despite being on an incredulous journey that had tested her on all accounts, this Princess was in no hurry to return home. Before she went home, she took a detour to the Sufi shrine of Mu'in al-Din Chishti at Ajmer.[9] She was finally in Fatehpur Sikri by March 1952.

[9]Beveridge, Henry, *The Akbarnama of Abul Fazl,* Low Price Publications, 2010.

The departure of these women from usual convention—by travelling on their own and making such a long pilgrimage—is likely a one-off event in the history of the Mughal Empire.

Envoys from Akbar's court regularly met the troupe during their stay in Ajmer, and Akbar himself met Gulbadan at Khanwa (Rajasthan). That night, as the story goes, no one slept.[10] Gifts were exchanged, and one imagines their stories merging as the women recounted what they had seen and heard during their travels.

Gulbadan Begum's influence over Emperor Akbar was undeniable. Father Antonio Monserrate, a Portuguese priest who travelled to Akbar's court, noted this too. He has written that when Gulbadan Begum returned from Mecca, 'the King had the street-pavements covered with silken shawls, and conducted her himself to her palace in a gorgeous litter, scattering largess meanwhile [sic] to the crowds'.[11]

As mentioned previously, the little we know about Gulbadan is from her own accounts (mostly from the time Akbar became the emperor). Akbar had immense respect for education, literature and arts. He would surround himself with scholars. His mother and Gulbadan

---

[10]Begam, Gulbadan, *The Humayun Nama,* Annette S. Beveridge (trans.), Royal Asiatic Society, 1902.

[11]Monserrate, Antonio, *The Commentary of Father Monserrate: S.J., on His Journey to the Court of Akbar,* John S. Hoyland (trans.), Asian Educational Services, 1922.

had extensive libraries, yet the attempts to teach Akbar to read came up short.

Some scholars insinuate that the King may have been dyslexic[12] but it is believed that he remembered everything that was read to him. He had people read to him almost every evening.

Despite his personal disinterest towards reading, Akbar was a man who treasured knowledge. And since he did not keep accounts, like Babur, he issued an order in 1587 asking a chosen few to document the rise of the Mughals in Hindustan. Gulbadan Begum was among the chosen ones. She was the only woman to be given this responsibility. She was 64 when this order was issued. Gulbadan's writings came from her memories alone and she also spoke to those who were older than her to get her stories right.

Her account begins with these words: 'In the name of God, the Merciful, the Compassionate.'

She then continues:

> There had been an order issued: 'Write down whatever you know of the doings of Firdous-Makani (Babur) and Jannat-Ashyani (Humayun).' At the time when His Majesty Firdaus-Makani passed from this perishable world to the everlasting home I, this

---

[12]Kumar, Anu, 'How Akbar Came to Love Books though He Never Learnt to Read', *Scroll.in,* 7 November 2015, https://tinyurl.com/2yjrb3eu. Accessed on 30 April 2023.

> lowly one, was eight-years-old, so it may well be that I do not remember much. However, in obedience to the royal command, I set down whatever there is that I have heard and remember.[13]

According to Ruby Lal, as a witness to an empire in the making, Gulbadan accepted the responsibility of being the first female chronicler at the Mughal court. How fascinating it would have been to also read Gulbadan's experiences from the time she went to Mecca; of her varied interactions with people she met; and her observations of a foreign land.

Gulbadan's *Humayun Nama* is priceless as she shares crucial stories there. It is here that she documents the death of her father. It is in this record that she describes how they mourned for him. It is here that she paints an intimate portrait of her father with her words, even managing to document his playfulness.

According to Gulbadan, after the Battle of Panipat, Babur got a gold coin minted weighing 'three imperial sers, that is 15 sers of Hind'. He had told Khwaja Khan to carry this heavy, freshly-minted gold back to Kabul and give it to Asas (his court jester). [14]

On Babur's orders, a hole was bored into the coin to enable a string to be slipped through it. The coin

[13]Begam, Gulbadan, *The Humayun Nama,* Annette S. Beveridge (trans.), Royal Asiatic Society, 1902.
[14]Ibid.

was then hung around the jester's neck. He was to be blindfolded before being given the coin. Gulbadan has mentioned how Asas grew increasingly worried about the weight around his neck till he finally felt the coin with his hands. He then danced around in joy, repeating over and over again, 'No one shall take away this *ashrafi* (gold coin) from me. No one!'[15]

According to Ruby Lal, a historian, her memoir follows no structure of writing prevalent at the time.[16] It wasn't something from the 'mirror of princes' genre which was essentially a guideline of how they should conduct themselves. It wasn't a record of the endless weddings, births and deaths that marked their extensive network of families. She broke away from how writers of her time wrote and were expected to write. She created a manuscript that details the everyday lives of those in the Mughal Empire. She also wrote about the changing seasons; the rivers and mountains that marked the land; as well as the customs and arts that defined it.

In one account, Gulbadan talks about the time Humayun had fallen ill. Maham Begum had then gone to the emperor and said to him, 'You are an emperor: What grief do you have? You have other children. My grief is that I have but one son.' To this Babur had replied, 'Although I have other sons, I love none as I love Humayun. It is

---

[15]Ibid.

[16]Lal, Ruby, *Domesticity and Power in the Early Mughal World*, Cambridge University Press, 2005.

for his sake that I have acquired empire, and I want the world to be bright for my beloved Humayun.'[17]

One can only imagine if Gulbadan felt uncomfortable knowing that her father and her adoptive mother favoured Humayun over her and all their siblings, but she never expresses these feelings in her writings. Humayun was the heir and that was it.

In her account, Gulbadan noted how Babur walked around Humayun's bed and uttered these words, 'O God! If a life may be exchanged for a life, I who am Babur, I give my life and my being for Humayun.' She also mentions in the book that, Babur fell ill that very day, and Humayun was well enough to pour water on his head and also give an audience to others.

Gulbadan's memoir acts as a record of the unrest during her father's and brother's reign, but there's more to it than just that. It's a faithful telling of events during her time—events that not only shaped her life, but also had lasting consequences on the Mughal Empire.

'The facts are as stated here… I have set down of good and bad whatever is known,' says Babur in a journal he used to keep, now known to the world as *Baburnama.*[18] It's considered to be one of the earliest and finest records of autobiographical literature. Out of his many children, it was Gulbadan who made her mark in literature.

---

[17]Ibid.

[18]Hiro, Dilip, *Baburnama: Journal of Emperor Babur,* Penguin Books, 2006.

She was a witness to an emerging monarchy and documented her learnings either in the *Humayun Nama* or in the *Ahval-i-Humayun Badshah* (which can be translated as 'conditions during the reign of Emperor Humayun'). It is as much an account of the domesticities of the Mughal household, as it is a record of Humayun's reign.

Gulbadan's work gives readers a unique insight into the inner workings of a world that stumped historians and foreign travellers. In one section, Gulbadan writes about Maham Begum's tenacity to get a grandson. As Humayun's mother, she wanted to assure a clear line of succession and secure her family's claim to the throne. According to Gulbadan, Maham Begum then convinced her son to wed Mewa Jan (the daughter of one of Maham Begum's courtly attendants). Historian Harbans Mukhia has mentioned that this was long before Akbar's birth.[19]

Just a few days after Humayun married Mewa Jan, Bega Begum (one of Humayun's favourite wives) came back from Kabul and announced that she was pregnant. After Bega Begum gave birth to a daughter named Aqiqa Begum (the same girl lost in the battle with Sher Shah), Maham Begum was convinced that her next grandchild would be a son. Undoubtedly, the woman who would give Humayun a male heir would see her status greatly elevated at the Mughal court. Great preparations were made in anticipation of the coming of the male heir.

[19]Mukhia, Harbans, *The Mughals of India*, John Wiley & Sons, 2008.

But 11 months later, there was no sign of any baby. At this point, Mewa Jan tried convincing people that it sometimes took a whole year for a baby to come. Her ruse was exposed but it got everyone's attention for as long it had lasted. This story of internal politics comes to us only from Gulbadan's chronicle.

In the presence of Mughal historians who diligently noted the comings and goings of everyone at the Mughal court—the hunting trips and the battle for influence; the relatives lost and won; and the priests and traders who came from far off places—there's a glaring absence of women who speak, move and breathe. This gap has been bridged by Gulbadan Begum's work, to some extent.

Gulbadan was a senior, pious Mughal woman. But her own social ranking, or the perception of how she'd be seen, didn't stop her from writing about women having desires and voicing those desires. For instance, she has documented the exchanges between the emperor and his wives.

One time, Bega Begum rebuked her husband for not seeing her enough and for choosing to spend time with his aunts instead. According to the *Humayun Nama,* she said: 'For days now, you've been visiting this (common) garden and haven't come to our house on a single one of those days. Thorns have not been planted on the way to our house.'[20]

[20]Begam, Gulbadan, *The Humayun Nama,* Annette S. Beveridge (trans.), Royal Asiatic Society, 1902.

Bega Begum was one of the women who had accompanied Gulbadan on her pilgrimage. She was also the one who, after Humayun's passing, mourned her husband by funding and supervising the construction of Humayun's Tomb. This garden-mausoleum continues to be one of Delhi's most celebrated and recognized architectural icons.

Though several Turkish words occur in records as it was her native tongue, the records are mostly in Persian. The use of Persian marked her as a 'learned' person.[21]

Gulbadan's writing and her intimate portrayal of the Mughal harem requires popularizing, in order to dispel the belief that the harem was only a place for beautiful young women.

Kishori Saran Lal, a medieval historian, writes this in his book *The Mughal Harem*:

> The term 'Mughal harem' conjures up a vision of a sequestered place ensconcing beautiful forms in mysterious magnificence in which sex orgies dominated or the master bargained for beauty and love on occasions... Naturally, every lady of consequence tried to win the master's undivided love and openly competed to gain ascendancy in the harem... These may be classed under the generic term jealousy. But on this, we need not dwell much

[21]Lal, Ruby, 'Historicizing the Harem: The Challenge of a Princess's Memoir', *Feminist Studies*, Vol. 30, No. 3, 2004.

> for the harem was not meant for the old and ailing. It was meant to be a bright place, an abode of the young and beautiful, an arbour of pleasure and retreat for joy.

If Gulbadan's text had been consulted for references to the harem, historians who had previously pegged the harem only as a dwelling for the young would have also read how Humayun would visit the gardens and spend time in the company of not just his wives but also his sisters, stepmothers and aunts. Gulbadan had written, 'All of us, the begums and my sisters, were in his society. When he went to any begum's or sister's quarters, all the begums and all his sisters used to go with him.'[22]

The harem may have become a more closed off place in Akbar's time,[23] but it was by no means cut off from the politics and functionings of the 'outside' world.

Gulbadan's writing is a collection of insightful snippets that have long been overlooked. For example, she writes that when one of Humayun's wives chided him for not visiting earlier, he replied: 'I am an opium addict, and if it takes me a long time to come to see you don't get cross.'[24]

---

[22]Begam, Gulbadan, *The Humayun Nama*, Annette S. Beveridge (trans.), Royal Asiatic Society, 1902.
[23]Lal, Ruby, 'Historicizing the Harem: The Challenge of a Princess's Memoir', *Feminist Studies*, Vol. 30, No. 3, 2004.
[24]Begam, Gulbadan, *The Humayun Nama*, Annette S. Beveridge (trans.), Royal Asiatic Society, 1902.

Gulbadan has also written of the time her father was building a pool in Dholpur, near Agra. He apparently told her, 'When this pool is ready, I'll fill it with wine.' Such a pool wouldn't have completely been out of the ordinary for Babur. He is believed to have been fond of baths as well as wine, so it is quite possible he'd think of combining the two.

However, Gulbadan later said that 'since he gave up wine before the battle with Ranga Sanga, he filled it instead with lemon sherbet'.[25] A bathhouse in the ruins where the octagonal pool was described to be located has been discovered.

Gulbadan's writing dispels the mystique surrounding the harem, and helps one see the realities of Mughal women's day-to-day lives. She noted how, when Humayun would come to visit one of his wives or his aunts, the ladies would initially follow an order of precedence. But as they chatted away for long hours, often well into the night, all sense of decorum was thrown out of the window. They'd just sleep anywhere instead of going back to their quarters. This scene that Gulbadan describes—of a world long gone by—could easily fit into modern-day portraits of any family or friends' gathering.

Gulbadan also talks of the time the ladies in the harem made plans to travel from Balkh to Laghman (in Afghanistan) to see the first rhubarb sprouting in the

---

[25]Ibid.

hills. The plan was to travel by moonlight. The women took so long to get ready that by the time they reached, the rhubarb leaves had already sprouted. Miffed at having missed the sight, an angry Humayun is said to have made the women write letters apologizing to him.

Such commonplace episodes of drama are largely missing from mainstream history. Gulbadan's approach to chronicling history, without weaving mighty tales of conquest, is a rare breed of writing. It needs no grandiose embellishments. One account of hers just talks of the time Hamida Banu sent nine sheep to each of their quarters. Another story talks about how once they were delayed by an hour during their travels with Humayun, after one of them slipped off the horse and fell into a river. She writes about trips where they had provisions—such as curd, sherbet, milk and so on—when they went to see a waterfall. She also writes about Humayun's penchant for orchards and growing oranges, and how he'd go up mountain passes just to see these orange orchards.

There's another story that notes how Hamida Banu had initially refused to marry Humayun. When Hamida was asked to come to Dildar Begum's (Gulbadan's mother) quarters on Humayun's insistence, Gulbadan notes her saying, 'If it is to pay my respects, I was exalted by paying my respects the other day. Why should I come again?'

Hamida Banu refused to see Humayun for well over a month, following which Dildar Bano had to approach her again. She tried convincing her by saying that someday she would marry someone, so 'who better than a King?' According to Gulbadan's records, Hamida Banu responded saying, 'Oh yes, I shall marry someone; but he shall be a man whose collar my hand can touch, and not whose skirt it does not reach.' Hamida is said to have talked of appropriate protocol and acceptable behaviour, saying: 'To see the King once is lawful; a second time this is forbidden. I shall not come.'[26]

Hamida Bano's reluctance to meet Humayun led him to say that if she wasn't agreeing, 'we will make her a consort'.[27] Having consulted the stars, for Humayun was keen on astrology, the two ended up getting married after all. Clearly, neither Humayun or Akbar could censor Gulbadan's work.

This portrayal of Hamida—as a woman who knew what she wanted—exists because Gulbadan documented it without fearing the consequences. She did not worry about what effect it would have on the readers and how it would affect how people remembered Humayun. She also did not worry about whether Akbar would object to either of his parents being portrayed this way. The fact that Humayun would approach his stepmother Dildar Begum for counsel on matters that were personally sensitive, like marriage and progeny, also showcases that

[26]Ibid.
[27]Ibid.

the Emperor cared about what the senior women at the Mughal court thought.

It is through Gulbadan that we hear the voices of the women in the Mughal court. It is through her documentations that we know that Mughal women were not subservient beings living for the pleasure of the emperor alone. Instead, her work shows how the Mughal emperors were moulded by their relationships with these women. Gulbadan's account is not a filtered version of history; it's a raw recollection of the events that left an impression on her and shaped an empire.

Much like her father, Babur, Gulbadan was mindful about honouring women by mentioning their names in context of births, instead of just mentioning them in context of their children. She lived in a time when there was legacy of erasures. Many times, women who bore a son destined to continue his father's name and fortunes, were themselves left nameless. Gulbadan herself has not been given her due for being the first female documentarian of the Mughal court.

In February 1603, when the cold winds from the north had not yet given way to spring, Gulbadan began to feel feverish. If one's life really flashes before the eyes embracing the eternal sleep, Gulbadan must have seen glimpses of a Mughal Empire.

Hamida Banu was by her side till the very end. Hamida Banu called out to Gulbadan, calling her 'Jiu' (Hamida's nickname for Gulbadan), but Gulbadan gave no response.

Then Hamida Banu called her by her name, 'Gulbadan!' At this, the Begum opened her eyes and muttered with her last few breaths, 'I die—may you live.'[28] After a life filled with advdentures and storytelling, she died at the age of 80.

Out of respect for Gulbadan, Akbar is also said to have carried her bier for some distance. Some believe that Akbar sorely missed his aunt and continued to talk about her till his own death in 1605. She lies buried in the same complex as her father, in modern-day Kabul. Like in life, here too, she was away from her husband. The references made to Gulbadan in the third volume of *Akbarnama* is yet another sign of the prestige and honour she enjoyed in the Mughal household.

Much of what we know of Gulbadan Begum comes to us from the works of Annette Susannah Beveridge, a British Orientalist. She translated *Humayun Nama* from Persian to English. The manuscript was originally a part of a collection of a thousand manuscripts in the collection of Colonel George William Hamilton. He had gathered these together during his tenure in Delhi and Lucknow.[29] The manuscripts were sold to the British Museum in 1868 after he passed away. And this is where Beveridge found it, battered and forgotten, lying in a land where

---

[28]Beveridge, Henry, *The Akbarnama of Abul Fazl,* Low Price Publications, 2010.

[29]Begam, Gulbadan, *The Humayun Nama,* Annette S. Beveridge (trans.), Royal Asiatic Society, 1902.

only a select few could understand the language it was written in.

'Princess Rose-body has rendered one essential service to history, by giving precise details of relationships in her own and contemporary families,'[30] Beveridge wrote shortly after having translated Gulbadan's work. *Humayun Nama* was published in English for the first time in the early 1900s. Up until then, no use had been made of the insights provided by Gulbadan. Owing to this trend of being neglected both in India and Europe, Beveridge refers to Gulbadan's work as a literary *parda-nashin* (something covered or hidden).

Unfortunately, the last pages of the manuscript are missing. Beveridge tried searching for a second copy of Gulbadan's book. The search went on for two decades with no end in sight. Till date, no other copy of the book has ever been found.

The story Gulbadan was narrating when the book abruptly goes quiet is one where Prince Kamran Mirza had been blinded by Humayun, after a feud that had lasted between the brothers for eight years. She says: 'The Emperor gave an order to Sayyid Muhammad, "Blind Mirza Kamran in both eyes." Sayyid went at once and did so. After the blinding, his Majesty the Emperor....'[31]

This is how Princess Gulbadan's account abruptly

---

[30]Ibid.

[31]Begam, Gulbadan, *The Humayun Nama*, Annette S. Beveridge (trans.), Royal Asiatic Society, 1902.

stops—about four years before Humayun tumbled down the stairs and almost six years before she finally made her way to Akbar's time. This sole copy of this manuscript now lies in the British Museum.[32]

Scattered among old, forgotten possessions in an attic or in a collection locked away from all eyes—if you find yellowed pages among jade bowls, dear reader, approach them with grace and care. Even though they might not be the lost pages of Gulbadan's manuscript, you might chance upon records that are an explorer's dream come true—records that could potentially change how we view those that came before us.

[32]Mukherjee, Siddhartha, 'When Women Meet After Eons', *Farbound.net*, 26 December 2017, https://tinyurl.com/yhts73zy. Accessed on 30 April 2023.

Velu

Avenger Incarnate

SIVAGANGA, 1772

Over 200 years ago, on the time-tested land now known as Tamil Nadu, a young woman called Udaiyal was walking with her cattle. As she grazed her cattle, Udaiyal heard the gallop of horses headed towards her. The sounds of the horses kicking up dry dust reached her much before she saw them. She was unprepared for who she was about to meet, or what would follow after.

Udaiyal may have been someone far removed from the affairs of the royal court but she instantly recognized who she had crossed paths with. On the horse, in front of her, was Velu Nachiyar. She was a woman whose talents in warfare and aptitude for martial arts were the stuff of legend. She was the Princess of Ramnad, a princess who was brought up with every skill a prince possessed. She was the princess who had gone on to become the Queen of the land Udaiyal belonged to—Sivaganga.

It was immediately clear to Udaiyal that Velu Nachiyar wasn't out just touring the empire. Accompanying the Queen was her young daughter and the Marudhu brothers. These two men had served the throne for a long time, and had slowly gone up the ranks. Udaiyal had no idea what these people were riding away from but it was clear to her that it was nothing pleasant.

Udaiyal was told that the British had attacked. Sivaganga had fallen. Udaiyal stood there in shock. She composed herself and professed her loyalty to the Queen. Then, they sped off again. That was the last time Udaiyal would ever see her Queen.

She didn't have much time to dwell on this strange encounter, as another dust cloud began to rise in the distance. More people were coming on horseback, most likely in pursuit of the Queen. As the sound of hooves came closer, Udaiyal realized the enemy had arrived. The hunt for Velu Nachiyar had begun. This hunt has been documented and passed down through oral stories.

VELU'S STORY

About 48 km from Madurai, in modern-day Tamil Nadu, stands the city of Sivaganga. One imagines temple bells ring all day long here and the smell of incense follows you across the city. It's bustling and lively—far removed from the bloodshed that the land has witnessed in its long and tumultuous history.

The city of Sivaganga is almost 300 years old. It was founded in 1730 by King Sasivarna Periyavudaya Thevar. For decades, before Sasivarna's time, Sivaganga (or Sivangangai) was part of the larger kingdom of Ramanathapuram (also known as Ramnad). This kingdom was eventually broken down into smaller halves, one of which was Sivaganga.

About 16 years after Sasivarna first became the King of Sivaganga, his son Muthuvaduganathaperiya Udaiyathevar married Velu Nachiyar. She was the daughter of the then King of Ramnad, Chellamuthu Sethupathy. Theirs was a dynasty in which women of royal birth were given the title of 'Nachiyar'. The men were called 'Sethupathy'—protectors of the sethu. The 'sethu' here refers to the fabled bridge that Lord Ram built from Rameswaram to Ravana's Lanka to help Hanuman's army cross over.

Born in the same year as the Sivaganga, Princess Velu came into the world on 3 January 1730. She was the only child of her parents. As heir to her father's throne, the Princess was surrounded by tutors who taught her skills expected of any true blood royal of her time. Velu was only 10 when her mother passed away. She grew up spending much of her time studying various languages and Sangam literature—the storehouse of Tamil history of the kingdoms before her time.

But her knowledge went beyond the learning tucked into literary works. The Princess excelled in *silambam*, an ancient form of martial arts that she had read about in the Sangam manuscripts. She was adept at using the *valuri*, a boomerang-like weapon crafted out of iron. She also won local armed combat championships and rode horses that she had tamed herself. She was also fluent in seven languages, including Urdu and French.[1]

The Princess was married to Muthuvaduganathaperiya when she was 16. Four years later, the Princess' husband became the King after Sasivarna died. With his ascension in 1750, Velu became the Queen of Sivaganga.

∽

History, especially the kind that is orally passed down from one generation to another, often tends to have twists and turns that border on being unbelievable. But that's exactly what rousing legends are made of—a balance between what we believe credible and the seemingly

---

[1]Garodia Gupta, Archana, *The Women Who Ruled India: Leaders. Warriors. Icons.*, Hachette India, 2019.

impossible. There's one such unbelievable story about Velu Nachiyar as well. And like all oral stories which can get embellished with time, this one should also be taken with a pinch of salt.

It is believed that once when the King and Queen were passing through the forests of Courtallam, a place whose calming waterfalls still draw in large crowds, they paused to rest for a bit, unaware that something was watching them from behind the forest greens. A tiger had them in its sights. The King was apparently his chosen meal for the day. Even as the tiger prepared to attack, Velu Nachiyar spotted his striped form and leapt into action.

If local accounts are to be believed—she is said to have caught hold of the tiger by its tail, jumped on it and killed it.[2] Embellished though the story may be, in all variations of the story Velu Nachiyar is the one who saves the King from the tiger.

∽

Life-altering things were happening outside of Sivaganga. Wars were being won and lost, and merchants were coming to the land in huge ships to build a kingdom under the guise of trade. But away from all that, there was peace inside the walls of the kingdom.

---

[2]Ibid.

The winds were changing beyond the delineated borders of their fruitful land. The price of being in power is to live with the heavy knowledge that peace, like war and misery, is a fleeting thing.

Outside their kingdom, the forces of the French, the Dutch and the English were all battling for economic and political influence over the region. These foreign forces were not just waging wars with native rulers, but were also engaged in a battle with each other. One imagines that the stakes were high, and unrest in the region kept spreading until it reached Sivaganga's borders as well.

Sivaganga's army was likely strong enough to keep some enemies from other kingdoms from waging an all-out war. However, as in any political landscape, the king's men knew that there would always be people inside the kingdom too who wished to overthrow Muthuvaduganathaperiya and oust all those who supported him. It helped that the kingdom had its staunch loyalists who had sworn to protect the throne.

Among these loyalists were Thandavarayan Pillai and the Marudhu brothers. Pillai was also the prime minister during Muthuvaduganathaperiya's father's time and he continued in this position when Muthuvaduganathaperiya took over. The two Marudhu brothers, Periya and Chinna, were the ones who chiefly commanded the king's army.[3]

---

[3]Kumar, Madhan, *Thamizh Is Not Just a Language: The Valour*, Educreation Publishing, 2017.

For many years, Velu Nachiyar's life and the throne were safe. Life was more or less predictable and routine, as routine as affairs of the court could be. And then, almost in the blink of an eye, everything seemed to fall apart.

ഗ

The person who acted as the catalyst in Velu Nachiyar's tale of tragedy was the Nawab of Arcot, Muhammad Ali Wallajah. Also known as the Nawab of Carnatic, Wallajah had been simmering with rage following Muthuvaduganathaperiya's ascension to Sivaganga's throne.

The Nawab saw himself as an overlord of smaller kingdoms such as Sivaganga; Velu Nachiyar's husband alleged that the Nawab had ascended the throne without his consent and blessings. Muthuvaduganathaperiya had also denied the Nawab the monetary tribute due to him. Such tributes were a way to ensure that smaller kingdoms were kept in line by those with larger territories. Not paying the requisite tribute could be seen as a challenge or as disrespect directed towards the Nawab.

The Nawab likely felt inclined to address the situation and to ensure that Muthuvaduganathaperiya paid for this alleged dishonour. If an example could be made of Sivaganga's king, it would also serve as a warning to all the rulers who thought of disobeying the Nawab. As he was an ally of the British, the Nawab knew he could count on their resources to establish his supremacy over Sivaganga.

Before proceeding further, we must take a step back here and examine the larger picture of the events afoot. Even before the British started swallowing up territories by applying the regressive policy of Doctrine of Lapse, they had ways of getting what they wanted.

Sivaganga's cordial relationship with the Dutch dated back to the time the kingdom was still a part of Ramnad; this had never gone down well with the British. When the Nawab approached them, seeking help in dealing with Sivaganga, the British saw a chance to fix what had been unnerving them.

Sivaganga was a small kingdom, but it did pose some threat to their growing trade. If the rulers of Sivaganga continued to trade with merchants of other countries, that would only result in continued competition from them. The Nawab, on the other hand, was a British ally who ruled over a majority of the northeastern part of modern-day Tamil Nadu. The British realized this was a win–win situation for them—a stellar way of killing two birds with a single stone.

When a messenger sent by the English approached the King with a proposal for a peaceful resolution, Muthuvaduganathaperiya embraced the idea. Thinking that the British would take time to mediate, he let his guard down. This proved to be a costly, irreparable mistake. The troops of the Nawab of Arcot and a battalion of the EIC then marched towards Sivaganga.

Led by two British officers (Joseph Smith and

Abraham Bonjour), the troops travelled many miles under an unforgiving sun to get to Sivaganga.[4] They had no intention of showing mercy to anyone who got in their way. In June 1772, the battalion finally reached Sivaganga. They attacked the kingdom from two sides for a greater chance at victory.

When the invading army reached there, Muthuvaduganathaperiya was in the town of Kalayarkoil. He was visiting a temple along with his second wife, Gowri Nachiyar. Velu Nachiyar and their daughter Vellachi were in the neighbouring town of Kollangudi.

It's not hard to imagine how the scene was likely played out. Given Sivaganga's location in South India, it was likely to have been warm when the King and his second wife were shot down. The King was dead. Sivaganga had fallen. To maximize their chances, the enemy's forces would have attacked suddenly and in full force. Caught unawares, the bullets that would have rained from different sides most likely killed not just the royals but also many innocent bystanders within a matter of minutes.

The Nawab of Arcot was but a pawn in the game of divide and conquer that the English had begun to master in India. But, for the time being, Sivaganga was under his control. With British soldiers and the Nawab's men

[4]Garodia Gupta, Archana, *The Women Who Ruled India: Leaders. Warriors. Icons.*, Hachette India, 2019.

crawling all over Sivaganga's territory, the kingdom was no place for a recently widowed Queen and her daughter. Both of them could challenge the Nawab's claim to the throne. So, along with the Marudhu brothers and Prime Minister Pillai, Velu Nachiyar and Vellachi left to find refuge.

Velu Nachiyar had a long road ahead of her. Many people were still loyal to the Queen. Udaiyal was one of them, though it isn't clear who she really was. Some believe that Udaiyal was one of the Queen's bodyguards who stayed back to give the Queen a head start and to delay the enemies trying to track her. Others believe that Udaiyal was a common citizen, shepherding cattle when she crossed paths with Velu Nachiyar.[5] Since these are oral histories narrated from one generation to another, it's hard to gauge which version is closest to the truth. Regardless of who Udaiyal was before that momentous day—bodyguard or shepherdess—all versions of the story end the same way. When forces of the British came looking for Velu Nachiyar, Udaiyal refused to reveal the Queen's location. She also refused to give them an idea of which direction she rode off in.

She stood her ground even when they threatened to hurt her. When the British realized that she wouldn't help them, they beheaded Udaiyal. Miles away from all

---

[5]Kumar, Madhan, *Thamizh Is Not Just a Language*, Educreation Publishing, 2017.

the bloodshed in Sivaganga, Velu Nachiyar continued to ride on. Along with her daughter, she had a small band of loyalists who had left the city with her.

They crossed fields and forests in their quest for refuge and finally found a safe haven at Virupaksha, a place governed by Gopal Nayak, also known as Gopal Naiyaker or Naicker, who was a patriot himself. Nayak was the polygar—a local administrative and military head—of Virupaksha. Stories of how he supported those fighting against the threat of foreign domination were aplenty; importantly, Velu Nachiyar finally had a place to rest.[6]

The struggle for freedom is no man or woman's sole charge, and the role played by people such as Nayak and Udaiyal—who stood firm despite the growing strength of the British—is as significant as the tales of famous leaders of India.

The Queen was distraught over the loss of her husband, people and land. One can only imagine the shock, and perhaps anger, that the now-deposed Queen felt when news of Udaiyal's execution reached her ears. As the oral stories go, this killing only further strengthened her resolve to ensure that Sivaganga had not lost its people in vain.

Life is a hard teacher and all of us must, at some time or another, learn that grief is a bitter pill. In this case, it's likely that Velu Nachiyar channelled that grief

---

[6]'Veerupakshi Gopal Naiyaker', *Azadi ka Amrit Mahotsav*, https://tinyurl.com/bdhwhrka. Accessed on 23 June 2023.

of losing her people and her home into something that could keep her going forward. Maybe some part of her felt she owed it to her daughter and her people to keep going. Maybe she owed it to herself, too.

For close to eight years, Velu Nachiyar stayed in hiding—biding her time as she attempted to forge new alliances. Often, this meant devising new strategies. With Prime Minister Pillai and the Marudhu brothers by her side, the Queen steadily built up a network of sources still loyal to the rightful heir of Sivaganga's throne.

As any royal trained to be a statesperson from their early days, it's likely that Velu knew well enough that just having spies wouldn't do the trick. So, she had Pillai draw up extensive plans while the Marudhu brothers trained men for battle. Along with learning traditional close combat and use of weapons such as the boomerang-like valari, the men also prepared themselves for using weapons that would redefine the future of wars—guns. Very likely, they also learnt the tactics of guerrilla warfare, lest the British spot them earlier than intended.

Velu Nachiyar wasn't content with these strategies alone. She was a skilled warrior just like her guard, Kuyili. Under the Queen's supervision, Kuyili trained an army of her own—a battalion of all-women soldiers who would fight alongside the men when the time came.

One reason why people still honour Velu Nachiyar is because of the commitment she showed to them. Here was a Queen who valued the lives of her people and recognized their sacrifices and loyalty. A testament to this was that the Queen's contingent of all-women warriors was named after Udaiyal.

Velu Nachiyar knew that reclaiming Sivaganga would be tough. Not only was the kingdom constantly under the watch of British forces, but there had also been consistent efforts to change the kingdom's course of history. In fact, under the new administration, it wasn't even known as Sivaganga anymore. It had been renamed as 'Hussain Nagar'.[7] The Nawab's son, Amir-ul-Umara, was now the ruling authority there on behalf of his father.

Despite these hurdles, Velu Nachiyar spent her days working on plans to reclaim Sivaganga. As a resourceful woman, she knew the importance of allies and spent time seeking them out. It was likely this resourcefulness that sealed the cordial relations she had with Hyder Ali, the Sultan of Mysore, besides the fact they had a common enemy.

The Sultan's relationship with the British had steadily been on the decline, long before Velu Nachiyar came into the picture. The Sultan of Mysore had been trading with the French, who supplied him with artillery and arsenal in his fight against the British.[8]

The intermediary between Velu and the Sultan was Gopal Nayak. As time ran its course, Velu Nachiyar's band

---

[7]Garodia Gupta, Archana, *The Women Who Ruled India: Leaders. Warriors. Icons.*, Hachette India, 2019.

[8]Ibid.

of loyalists and Nayak convinced the Sultan to consider aiding the Queen. The Sultan agreed to meet the Queen and her aides at the Dindigul Fort.

Built in 1605, the fort was then under the kingdom of Mysore. It was a sturdy sanctuary on a towering hillock about 64 km from Madurai. Both parties likely agreed it would be a safe meeting spot, away from prying eyes and with enough places to fight back in case of a surprise attack.

When the Sultan arrived at the fort, expecting to find a woman surrounded by guards, he could not spot anyone. One can only imagine the annoyance the Sultan must have felt. He had travelled all the way for a meeting, only to find that the other person hadn't shown up.

But Velu Nachiyar was there, disguised as a man. This was likely an attempt to thwart British spies, if there were any in the vicinity. This was only one of the many surprises that came the Sultan's way that day. The Queen from a Tamil-speaking kingdom went on to converse with him in flawless Urdu. She spoke the language as if it was her own, and the Sultan took note of this considerate gesture.

It is likely that by the end of this meeting, Velu Nachiyar had the Sultan's admiration and his whole-hearted support. He gave her 400 gold coins.[9] He also promised her ammunition and thousands of cavalry men, who would come armed with cannon balls when

[9]Ibid.

the time came for her to fight the British. By the time they left Dindigul, their friendship and support for each other was a done deal. Besides assistance with raising an army, he had also offered her the safety of staying in Dindigul Fort after all.

Caught between monitoring the ins and outs of the enemy forces in Sivaganga and vigorously training for battle while she raised a child, Velu Nachiyar was dealt another blow—she lost her devoted Prime Minister to old age. One assumes losses like this would have made her long for her homeland. She's likely to have craved the sights and smells of the home she was forced to flee. And besides all that, there was also the grief she had to constantly live with. This was not a self-imposed exile; she hadn't left by choice. So the weight of missing a place and people, some of whom were no longer around, is likely to have weighed heavily on her.

It's not clear how the Sultan found out that Velu had been yearning for her homeland. But oral stories indicate that when he caught wind of how much she missed home, he wanted to do something to lift her spirits. Velu Nachiyar had been pining to pay obeisance in the temple of Rajarajeshwari—the deity of the royal family. But the temple and the deity inside it were inaccessible to her in exile. So, the Sultan had his people fetch mud from the original temple in Sivaganga. This mud was brought to Velu Nachiyar and was used to build a small temple. This temple, with a handful of mud from her lost homeland, became a symbol that Velu Nachiyar held onto during her forced exile.

It took the Queen eight years to be confident that her new army was strong and equipped enough to face the enemy. In 1780, Velu Nachiyar set out to reclaim her kingdom. Her army boasted both men and women—many of whom were once forest dwellers. There were also a number of Muslim soldiers from the Sultan's army that rode alongside Velu Nachiyar's forces.

With Kuyili leading the women's brigade and the Marudhu brothers heading the men's contingent, Velu Nachiyar's march to reclaim her kingdom saw her entering into a series of battles at different places on their way to Sivaganga. They suffered losses but ended up winning the battles.

There's an oral story, narrated in parts of eastern India (modern-day Odisha), that the river Daya's water changed colour after the Kalinga War. A similarly striking visual has been passed down through oral stories about Velu Nachiyar's battle too. These local legends say that the river Vaigai turned red as the Queen's army marched towards their destination.

When they finally reached the outskirts of Sivaganga, some people from the villages poured in to join the Queen's army. It's likely that some people had been waiting and hoping for this day to come since the previous rulers were ousted after the violent shoot out many years ago.

The Queen's army is likely to have found it hard to breach the high walls that encompassed the place, especially in broad daylight. The only way to get to the heart of the kingdom was to have someone on the inside open the gates. This seemed unfeasible since the gates were closely guarded by the Nawab's men as well as British sentries. They had no one on the inside they could trust, as it could mean the difference between life and death.

Besides, they were aware of the possibility that the Nawab and the British were prepared for an attack. Word of the Queen's long march had most likely reached their ears. Pulling off a surprise attack seemed next to impossible.

There was another worrisome problem to deal with. Velu Nachiyar had been told that the British troops inside the gates had a well-stocked arsenal. They had explosives stockpiled at different places. One misstep could send forth multiple explosions. To win this battle, they needed more than brute force.

It was at this time that Velu Nachiyar and Kuyili came up with a plan that went a long way in cementing their fate. The festival of Vijayadashmi—the last day of Dusshera—was just around the corner. For decades together, it was a tradition for women from across the kingdom to gather in the main temple. This year wasn't going to be any different.

Velu and Kuyili likely saw this as the perfect opportunity

to gain access and enter the gates. No one would suspect a seemingly regular flock of female devotees.[10] After all their efforts, the last thing they had to do was disguise themselves and blend in with everyone. It was a gamble worth taking, but the rewards came with irreversible consequences.

Inside the temple premises, local custom dictated three rounds of worship for the Goddess Rajarajeshwari. As soon as they paid their respects to the Goddess, Velu Nachiyar's voice rang out over the tinkling of the temple bells. It was her war cry—a call that her army was awaiting. Her contingent of female warriors answered her call, while drawing forth their weapons. They launched into battle and fought for everything they loved.

The attack left the enemy soldiers stunned. They would have likely expected an army to attack and for bullets to fly, but not for a small band of women to surprise them the way they did. By the time they recovered enough to retaliate, the women had already taken out a number of them. Amidst all the fighting, the women also managed to ring the temple bell. This was a sign that the gates of the fort had now been opened. The winds of change quickly moved in Velu Nachiyar's favour.

The rest of Velu Nachiyar's army—the men who had been waiting outside—stormed in. This was the moment

---

[10]Kurup, Pushpa, *Power Women: A Journey into Hindu Mythology, Folklore and History*, Bloomsbury India, 2018.

they had been dreaming of for eight long years.

The one thing that worked against Velu Nachiyar's army was the enemy's supply of rifles and ammunition. Her army only had a limited number of supplies since they had travelled far and had already fought battles along the way. Their initial surprise attack had helped, but it wasn't enough to fend off the strikes that followed. The enemy had too much ammunition within easy reach.

It seemed like they had been preparing for battle, or were ready to go to war at a moment's notice. Even as the war waged on, Velu Nachiyar and Kuyili realized that the only way to win for certain was to disrupt this supply of ammunition. But doing that seemed impossible, unless they won this battle. And by that time, it would have been too late for them to recover.

Kuyili stepped up at this point. She went back into the temple and found a pot brimming with ghee. This was the clarified butter meant to help light lamps in honour of the Goddess. Kuyili took the pot of ghee and doused herself in it. As the local stories go, Kuyili then ran into the ammunition warehouse and set herself on fire. The whole place is said to have blown up, taking down soldiers from both sides.

It is safe to assume that the day was marked by bloodshed and mourning, but between Kuyili's sacrifice and the persistence of Velu Nachiyar's army, she won the war and Hussain Nagar was Sivaganga again. The flag of Sivaganga, bearing the image of Hanuman, unfurled against blue skies eight years after it was taken down.

When the remaining enemy soldiers were rounded up and brought in front of Velu, among them were the officers of the British government. A senior officer realized that there was no escape for him, and he pleaded with Velu to spare his life. In return, he said, he'd speak in her favour and request the EIC to ensure that Sivaganga was left undisturbed in the future.

As one of her first acts as the reinstated Queen, Velu announced she had no intention of killing him. The victory was clearly hers and there was no need for more blood to be shed. 'We don't need your life or anything else from you,' the Queen told him. 'You are free to live here as a guest, but never as the owners of this land.'[11]

One assumes news of this victory would have quickly spread across the kingdom.

After she paid her respects and marked the contributions of those that died in her name, Velu Nachiyar finally took the throne.

According to Archana Garodia Gupta, Velu Nachiyar went on to rule Sivaganga for about 10 years. In 1790, the Queen passed on the throne to her daughter. In a varying account, the Marudhu brothers took over after Velu Nachiyar, writes Madhan Kumar. Other accounts, which seem to walk a fine line between these two, says

---

[11]Kumar, Madhan, *Thamizh Is Not Just a Language*, Educreation Publishing, 2017.

the throne was passed onto Vellachi, but was effectively taken away after she was wedded to a person of Marudhu brothers' choosing.

There's no proper documentation of Velu Nachiyar's passing. Hence, one must rely on the oral stories passed down through generations. Stories say that she fell ill after a while and went to Paris for treatment. While she was there, she is said to have given lessons in martial arts to a French aristocrat's daughter. Details of her stay in Paris remain unknown and largely undocumented.

After she returned to Sivaganga, she only stayed there for a short while. Instead, she is said to have spent the remainder of her days in Virupaksha Palayam—the place that granted her refuge when she needed it most; the place where she had nursed her spirits after losing everything; the place where she built her army of friends and supporters. And here, on 25 December 1796, Velu is said to have breathed her last at the age of 66.

When the tales of her valour are spoken, people call her 'Veeramangai' Velu Nachiyar. The Tamil moniker 'Veeramangai' translates to 'brave woman'. This Queen had lost and reclaimed her kingdom almost 50 years before Manikarnika, the all too familiar Rani of Jhansi, was even born.

Despite living a life that stands as a testament to great strength and sense of duty, Velu Nachiyar hasn't got her due. When the country recounts the heroes and heroines of India's history, her name rarely comes up.

Perhaps the most popular image one can find of the Queen who became a warrior is the one on the stamp issued in 2008. On this tiny stamp, Velu Nachiyar stands poised for action holding a partially sheathed sword. A feathered turban keeps her long, dark hair in place, and draped over her blue sari is a gold sash. It is this photo—a product of creative liberty—which commemorates Velu Nachiyar's efforts in an era of resistance long before the Revolt of 1857.

Some who know her story even refer to her as India's Joan of Arc. But this is an undue comparison. The fearless Joan of Arc, a remarkable heroine of France, was burned at the stake at the age of 19. Such comparisons only exist because Joan of Arc is a more popularly romanticized figure with many depictions in art and literature. Figures such as Velu Nachiyar have unfortunately remained on the sidelines, owing to a limited retelling of their equally rousing stories. Their valour and determination are, perhaps, the only common attributes between the two women.

When you read Velu Nachiyar's story, it is not just the bravery of a young woman that is remarkable. It is also the element of sisterhood, created by the way the Queen empowered women to band together and train as warriors to take up arms. Women were trained to protect her but they could stand on their own even in battle. There's an attempt on Velu Nachiyar's part to ensure that the ultimate act of sacrifice by Kuyili and Udaiyal (and women like them) were not forgotten, and that their contributions were not erased when the history of Sivaganga was recounted.

State leaders of Tamil Nadu pay floral tributes to Velu Nachiyar every year on 3 January, the anniversary of her birth. This was after the then Chief Minister J. Jayalalithaa instituted the ritual in 2014. Velu Nachiyar certainly deserves a greater role in the memory of the nation. Among the abundant number of annexations, conquests and occupations that marked the rise and fall of the British in India—Velu Nachiyar was one of the few rulers who managed to reclaim her kingdom from the grasp of the British.

In the heart of modern-day Sivaganga stands the dilapidated remains of the palace that was built by Velu's father-in-law. It was nearly three centuries ago when Sivaganga welcomed its first royals. The palace has since been plundered and left in shambles, once rebuilt and restored, and now forgotten.

Among the concrete remains that have stood the test of time is the temple of Rajarajeshwari. The palace may perhaps never reach the heights of its former glory days, but if you ever find yourself walking in the crowded lanes of Sivaganga, dear reader, remember the lives lived and lost to reclaim a kingdom. And before you press on ahead, pause by the bronze statue of Velu Nachiyar. It stands at the entrance of the palace, as if to show that the kingdom's protector is still watching over Sivaganga.

Amrit

Khadi with a Side of Tennis

SHIMLA, AUGUST 1942

During the Quit India Movement, a rising tide of dissent against the British had built up to an unmistakable crescendo. Nationalists from across the country had banded to disrupt the churnings of the government machinery.

Among these freedom fighters was a woman who would step out of her Shimla mansion every morning to lead the crowds raising anti-British slogans. She would be clad in khadi saris, and the marks on her body hinted that she had known violence at some point of her life.

Between 9 and 16 August 1942, processions led by

her were lathi charged at least 15 times.[1] Those who have documented the lathi charges describe them as being indiscriminate and ruthless. After several of these protest marches, this woman was arrested at Kalka and taken to Ambala Jail via road.

This Oxford-educated woman was permitted to carry her own bedding roll to prison. She also took a spinning wheel with her to continue weaving khadi, a brass bowl for drinking water, along with a copy of the Bible and the Bhagavad Gita. Pigeons and rats were her constant companions in the foul jail cells. The jail food and the environment behind those walls made her so ill that she had to be hospitalized just weeks after being imprisoned.

When she fell ill, the authorities sent her back to her Shimla home where she was placed under house arrest.

Days and nights merged into one another as she was largely cut off from the outside world. During this time of house arrest, she lost a brother. Even then, the letter she had written to her sister-in-law to console her was never sent.

This woman's life had taken several strange turns.

---

[1]Singh, Mohinder, *History and Culture of Panjab*, Atlantic Publishers and Distributors, New Delhi, 1989.

She had grown up with luxuries and had seen a world that only a select few could enter. Born into a world of opulence, she was now locked up in her own house after a stint in jail. She had chosen to switch a life of being driven around in motor cars with one of *padyatras* (journeys on foot) so she could campaign for the rights of the less privileged. She walked and walked. She spent so many hours under the hot Indian sun that the heat made her ill.

Despite her actions against the government and things growing tense between them, they still wanted her to represent them on the international stage. This was because the woman who fit in so easily among nationalist leaders was also a suave, well-educated person who could hold out on her own. This woman was Rajkumari Amrit Kaur, the firebrand Princess of Kapurthala (the former princely state of Punjab). The institutions built under her supervision continue to contribute to the functioning of modern India to this day.

AMRIT'S STORY

If the politics of today is considered corrupt, the events of yesteryears also win no laurels on moral grounds. Almost every king, queen and sultan looked out for themselves and responded to events keeping their interests first.

Take for instance, the history of Kapurthala. Maharaja Randhir Singh succeeded his father, Nihal Singh Sahib Bahadur, as the ruler of Kapurthala on 13 September 1852. His family had fought against the British for the Sikh kingdom, alongside the forces of Maharaja Ranjit Singh. But their alliances shifted, like sand dunes in a wind-dominated desert, and Randhir Singh sided with the British in 1857.[2]

For this show of support and loyalty to the British Empire, Randhir Singh was rewarded with large land grants in Uttar Pradesh (then known as the United Provinces of Agra and Awadh). This greatly added to the fortunes that their family already had in Punjab. This support also contributed in making Randhir Singh popular at Queen Victoria's court in England.

Randhir Singh's elder son, Kharak Singh Sahib Bahadur, succeeded him after he died on an ocean voyage to Europe in 1870. Harnam Singh was the new Maharaja's younger brother. The two brothers had a disagreement and Harnam Singh was 'banished' from Kapurthala; he went to live on their properties in Awadh and Jalandhar.[3]

This was allegedly his punishment for converting to Christianity. 'Grandfather changed his faith and forfeited forever his chances of acquiring the Kapurthala gaddi (throne),' writes Harnam Singh's grandson Billy Arjan

---

[2]Singh, Arjan, *The Legend of the Maneater*, Sangam Books, 1993.
[3]Ibid.

Singh in his book, *The Legend of the Maneater.* [4] However, in 1907, the British government made Harnam Singh 'a hereditary raja' and awarded him knighthood. He was also given the responsibilities of handling the family's properties in Awadh for a lifetime.[5]

Harnam Singh married Priscilla Golaknath in 1875.[6] Priscilla was a Bengali Christian who came to be known as Rani Priscilla Kaur Sahiba after their marriage. It is from this marriage—a coming together of inheritance lost and gained—that Rajkumari Amrit Kaur was born. She came into the world in British India's Lucknow on 2 February 1889—the same year that Jawaharlal Nehru was born in. Little did her parents know that she would fight for a free India alongside Nehru one day.

Her childhood was lined with every privilege one could think of as her family thrived. Apart from personal wealth, the Rajkumari's father also held many official designations. He was briefly a part of the Punjab Vidhan Sabha then.[7]

The Rajkumari's father had a temper that flared easily, a trait that highlights his passionate nature. The

---

[4]Ibid.

[5]'The Ahluwalia Dynasty', *RoyalArk*, https://tinyurl.com/3rcdmn82. Accessed on 23 June 2023.

[6]'Golaknath Memorial Church, Jalandhar: Religious Legacy Stands Tall', *The Tribune*, 25 April 2021, https://tinyurl.com/5tfytrhj. Accessed on 23 June 2023.

[7]Joshi, Shriniwas, 'The Gandhi Connection', *The Tribune*, 2007, https://tinyurl.com/sxvfd7a4. Accessed on 21 June 2023.

often-bloodshot eyes, that his grandson Billy Arjan Singh talks about in his book, were supposedly from the few pegs of fine Scotch he liked to have in the evenings. Perhaps, his passionate nature also made him likeable as he was well-favoured at Britain's court.

As mentioned in Billy Arjan Singh's book, those who knew him say that he had an exceptional presence and all of these titbits go into the making of a character. The authenticity of these stories, however, cannot be verified. One story goes that he had only lost one tooth by the time he turned 80, and that too was owing to an accident from years ago. He passed on some of this charm to his daughter as well, as she grew up to be a favourite in her many circles.

Harnam Singh had eight children. There was a ninth child as well who did not survive. The Rajkumari grew up with seven older brothers, including Billy Arjan Singh's father Kunwar Jasbir Singh. In such an environment, one can either grow up overly protected and sheltered from the world, or one turns out to be tough. The courage she exhibited throughout her life hinted she was the latter kind of person.

According to Rosalind Parr's book, in 1902, the Rajkumari accompanied her father to Britain when he was expected to attend the coronation of Edward VII. She was 12 at the time. She spent the next six years at the Sherborne School for Girls (a boarding school in Dorset, England). Much of the Rajkumari's early life was spent away from the country of her birth.

The events unfolding in the early years of our lives often have a large impact on who we grow up to be, even when we don't recall the details of the days.

The Rajkumari's days at Sherborne saw her growing up in a world where people of her social status were aplenty, but it's likely that she was also acutely conscious of her Indian heritage (considering her father's leanings towards Indian reformers like Gopal Krishna Gokhale).

No matter the path she chose for her future self, it is likely that she always had a life of security owing to her family's affluent background and social standing. But the way this Rajkumari turned all her luxuries into resources for her country was remarkable.

The Rajkumari's father was among the first Indian princes who sent their daughters abroad to study. Harnam Singh was educated by an American priest, Reverend J.S. Woodside, who was committed to the education of girls. Woodside went on to become one of the founders of the Woodstock Women's School and Teacher's Training College in Dehradun. Her father was also a member of the Lady Dufferin Fund, an organization that was formed to improve medical conditions for women in India. This organization also ensured that more women were trained as doctors, midwives and nurses.

The Rajkumari's mother, Priscilla Sahiba, was associated with the Young Women's Christian Association (YWCA)—an institution still committed to providing women access to safe hostels across the world. These influences manifested themselves in the Rajkumari as well.

It was likely in England that thc Rajkumari developed a lifelong love for sports. She became the captain of the hockey, cricket and lacrosse teams at her school while also carrying out her duties as the head girl. After school, her next stop was the University of Oxford.[8]

The Rajkumari was fluent in French and Italian and was a gifted pianist. She returned from Oxford at the age of 20.[9]

The Rajkumari also had an abiding love for tennis. And the game loved her back. After her return from Oxford, Amrit spent much of her time in Shimla. She won several tennis championships and attended social gatherings.

It's possible that when the Rajkumari came back to her home country, she may have had trouble adjusting to the lifestyle. Britain had its own rigid code of conduct for women, sure, but there may have been things the Rajkumari just could not come to terms with on her return to India. It is likely that it was these things that drew her to Mahatma Gandhi's teachings.

Outside the tennis court (that was almost like a home for the Rajkumari), India was on a slow boil. The voices of

---

[8]Bharadwaj, Deeksha, 'Rajkumari Amrit Kaur, the Princess Who Was Gandhi's Secretary & India's First Health Minister', *The Print*, https://tinyurl.com/3wxvwecs. Accessed on 23 June 2023.

[9]*Eminent Parliamentarians Monograph Series*, Lok Sabha Secretariat, 1993.

discontent against the British, owing to their questionable ways of administration and growing instances of brutality against Indians, were growing stronger and louder.

Harnam Singh kept the doors of his home open for the leaders of India's freedom movement, like Gopal Krishna Gokhale. Harnam Singh's meetings with these nationalist leaders had a lasting effect on the Rajkumari as she got to see firsthand how the tide of politics in India was turning. The Rajkumari later said that the flames of her passionate desire to see India free from foreign domination were fanned by these meetings her father hosted.[10]

The seed of patriotism sown by her father eventually led to the Rajkumari becoming a staunch Gandhian. The Rajkumari herself has said, 'I first heard of Gandhiji from Mr Gokhale who was a friend of my father's.' She also added how her father's house often served as a 'rendezvous' point for the leading Congressmen of the day.[11]

She first met Mahatma Gandhi in the winter of 1915–16 in Bombay (now Mumbai), when Congress was in session. His beliefs resounded with her, and a lifetime of correspondence through letters began.

---

[10]Roychowdhury, Adrija, 'Amrit Kaur: The Princess Turned Gandhian Who Fought Nehru on Women's Political Participation', *The Indian Express*, 2020, https://tinyurl.com/9k76ps77. Accessed on 23 June 2023.

[11]Gandhi, Mohandas, and Amrit Kaur, *Letters to Rajkumari Amrit Kaur*, Navajivan Publishing House, 1961.

Their relationship, based primarily on these letters, is well-documented in the book *Letters to Rajkumari Amrit Kaur.* Such was their correspondence that Gandhi, who previously would address her as 'Dear sister', over time began calling her 'idiot', 'rebel', etc. Gandhi would sign off these letters by referring to himself as 'tyrant', 'warrior' or even 'robber'.[12]

This was a time in India's history when the voices of dissent were beginning to echo everywhere. Government officers had also begun taking violent action against these protesters. Then came the event that shocked the nation to its core—the Jallianwala Bagh Massacre. On 13 April 1919, Acting Brigadier-General Reginald Dyer ordered his troops to indiscriminately open fire on an unarmed crowd in Amritsar's Jallianwala Bagh. The ensuing bloodshed left at least 400 people dead in the firing, with the toll rising up to 1,000 later.[13]

The British were the Rajkumari's friends, well-wishers, school and college mates, but what happened in Amritsar likely convinced her that colonial rule had to end.

The Rajkumari met Gandhi in Jalandhar soon after the Jallianwala Bagh massacre. It was then, in the aftermath of the massacre, that she expressed her desire to actively join Gandhi's fight against the British Empire. But her

[12]Ibid.

[13]'Jallianwala Bagh Massacre: What Happened to General Dyer after He Ordered Firing on Indians?', *The Indian Express*, 13 April 2023, https://tinyurl.com/2skzatdn. Accessed on 21 June 2023.

parents were hesitant in letting their only daughter step into this unpredictable, dangerous territory.

In the book *Letters to Rajkumari Amrit Kaur*, she has said: 'He (Gandhi) asked what my parents would feel about it (joining the ashram). I had to say that they would resent it. He then said, "You must not hurt them and you can work for me in your own environment without necessarily joining my ashram."'[14]

After her mother passed away in 1924, Gandhi spoke to the Rajkumari and stressed how, now more than ever, it was her duty to stay with her ageing father. And she did. By then she had already begun doing her part, without joining Gandhi at his ashram. She reorganized the work of the Punjab Spinners Association (PSA) and supported village industries in Jalandhar's five villages. Economic independence, she realized, was crucial in the new India that she wanted to see. Besides this, she also frequently travelled to support a cause particularly close to Gandhi's heart—the betterment of the lives of Dalits.

It's safe to say that the Rajkumari was acutely aware of whatever was happening around her, be it India's freedom struggle or the societal status of women everywhere. It is likely that because of this increased awareness, she wanted to actively do as much as possible to help make things better. She had always been a champion of equal rights; as time passed, she must have become more vocal

[14]Ibid.

about her beliefs. She campaigned against the purdah system as well as the *devadasi* tradition as well.

As a champion of female education and a vocal critic of child marriage, she once said: 'Child marriage is eating as a canker into the vitality of our national life. Girls become mothers while they are children themselves, and bring into the world off-springs, who are, in the very nature of things, the victims of disease and ill-health.'[15] Along with being a Gandhian and a freedom fighter, Amrit Kaur was also a staunch feminist who urged women everywhere to think and act for themselves.

In 1927, an Irish-Indian educationist called Margaret Elizabeth Cousins founded the All India Women's Conference (AIWC)—an organization for the welfare of women and children. The Rajkumari was one the key members of the organization for several years. One of the main goals of the AIWC was the demand for universal adult franchise—the right to vote for all adults, regardless of one's caste, class, race, gender or ethnicity.

The finest of India's women were part of this organization. Kamaladevi Chattopadhyay, the social reformer who is credited with bringing about a renaissance in Indian handlooms, was one of the first secretaries of this organization. Another notable member was the poet and political activist Sarojini Naidu.

---

[15]*Eminent Parliamentarians Monograph Series*, Lok Sabha Secretariat, 1993.

While appearing with a delegation of women in front of the Lothian Committee (constituted for responsible governance), the Rajkumari presented the case for universal adult franchise in 1932 and 1933. The idea was for women and men to be recognized as equals in all fields, with women also having the right to vote and hold office.

In the Rajkumari's own words: 'The mere obtaining of the power of the vote is not enough. [...] We must consider the basis of franchise; secondly, the methods employed for the exercise of the vote; and thirdly, the manner in which women are to be represented in the future councils of the country.'[16] While she recognized that the right to vote was significant, she also wanted to stress on how simply having that right did not guarantee women an equal say in the society.

By 1933, significant things were taking place on the international stage as well. Both Germany and Japan were withdrawing from the League of Nations. All of this was a precursor to the events that eventually sent the world reeling into the Second World War.

On the Indian stage, more and more women were joining the protest marches against the British Raj. This was a group that was fighting two wars at the time. One was the war for India's Independence, and the other was for them to be treated as equals to their male counterparts.

---

[16]Sharma, Kumud, *Power vs. Representation: Feminist Dilemmas, Ambivalent State and the Debate on Reservation for Women in India,* Occasional Paper 28, Centre for Women's Development Studies, 1998.

By 1935, there were many places in British India that had begun giving women the right to vote but only if they owned a certain amount of property. Besides the fact that this limited the right to vote only to privileged sections of society, there was another problem as well. Very few women owned property at that time. Considering this, only a tiny margin of women actually got to vote.

The Rajkumari was part of a small team that travelled to London to address the rights of Indian women in front of the Joint Parliamentary Franchise Committee.

The well-spoken Rajkumari's presentation in London was such a success that her group was extended an invitation to attend the League of Nations. That's how Indian women, draped in khadi saris, found themselves rubbing shoulders with world leaders in September 1933.

Besides gathering support for Indian women, this small band of women helped spread ideas in favour of Indian Independence. India now had a representation and an identity of its own on an international platform, spearheaded by women in khadi. Her campaign for equal rights and opportunities continued after the Rajkumari returned to India as well.[17]

In 1936, when Gandhi wanted more women to join the freedom struggle, he sought the Rajkumari's assistance. He wrote to her saying, 'I am now in search of a woman

---

[17]Parr, Rosalind, 'Solving World Problems: The Indian Women's Movement, Global Governance, and "The Crisis of Empire", 1933–46', *Journal of Global History*, Vol. 16, No. 1, March 2021.

who would realize her mission. Are you that woman, will you be one?'[18]

By that time, the Rajkumari's parents had passed away. Almost as if she was waiting for this letter all her life, she embraced a life of austerity without a second thought. She left behind her life of silk fineries and sumptuous durbars to spend an extended period of her life in Gandhi's Sevagram Ashram near Wardha, Maharashtra.

For about 16 years she worked as his English secretary; worked on the *Harijan* (a weekly newspaper edited by Gandhi); wove khadi; slept on the floor in a room she shared with many others; and washed her own plates and clothes. She also learnt Gujarati and practised her Hindi script. This globe-trotting, Oxford-returned woman was equally comfortable with her international identity as she was with her regional one.

When not writing letters or setting up meetings for women's rights, she spent hours weaving khadi on the *charkha* (spinning wheel). By this time, khadi had already emerged as a strong symbol for India's freedom movement.

The one reminder of her previous life that the Rajkumari held onto was tennis. In Gandhi's ashram, one had to abide by his set of strict rules. She convinced Gandhi to let her play tennis for an hour out of the several hours one was expected to spin the charkha. This

---

[18]Gandhi, Mohandas, and Amrit Kaur, *Letters to Rajkumari Amrit Kaur*, Navajivan Publishing House, 1961.

was an exception that Gandhi allowed, and the Rajkumari continued to play the sport at the ashram.[19]

In 1936, around the time she moved to the ashram, Jawaharlal Nehru was presiding over a session of the Indian National Congress. There was not a single woman on his list. The Grand Old Lady of Independence, Aruna Asaf Ali, recalled the Rajkumari's reaction to this in these words: 'Rajkumari was such an ardent believer in women's role in public life that she did not even hesitate to criticize Pandit Nehru on this score.'[20]

Like others working towards universal adult franchise, the Rajkumari strongly believed that there should be no reservations for women. She felt that if practical equality was secured for women in the domain of franchise, they would be able to find their way into the legislative and administrative institutions of the country without any special expedients.[21]

When Gandhi announced the Salt Satyagraha (Dandi March) in 1930, the Rajkumari was on the frontlines of the non-violent protest. She was arrested in Bombay for this.

---

[19]Bamzai, Kaveree, 'Princess of Hearts: India's First Health Minister Rajkumari Amrit Kaur', *India Today*, 25 September 2017, https://tinyurl.com/mr2yhvvd. Accessed on 23 June 2023.

[20]*Eminent Parliamentarians Monograph Series*, Vol. 15, Lok Sabha Secretariat, New Delhi, 1993.

[21]Roychowdhury, Adrija, 'Amrit Kaur: The Princess Turned Gandhian Who Fought Nehru on Women's Political Participation', *The Indian Express*, 2020, https://tinyurl.com/9k76ps77. Accessed on 23 June 2023.

As a representative of the Congress in the late 1930s, the Rajkumari once headed out on a goodwill mission to Bannu (now in the Khyber Pakhtunkhwa province of Pakistan). Her goal was to connect with the freedom fighters of the region. For this act of seeking out allies, the British government charged her with sedition on 16 July 1937. She was fined and imprisoned but carried on as if these things did not matter at all.

The Rajkumari's political leanings were always clear. And despite a background that distinguished her from others involved in the freedom struggle, the British government was well aware of her personal influence (both within and outside the country). This is why they had her appointed as a member of the Advisory Board of Education (ABE). The Rajkumari stepped down from this position when she joined the Quit India Movement in 1942.

She was also a big believer in keeping pace with what was happening elsewhere in the world and advocated that India be aware of international affairs for 'two successive world wars have shown that the actions of one nation have repercussions far beyond its neighbors'.[22] War was especially personal for her. She had lost one of her brothers, Captain Inderjit Singh, in Belgium during the First World War.

---

[22] *Woman with a Mission, Rajkumari Amrit Kaur: A Centenary Volume,* All India Women's Conference, University of California, 1989.

A dog called Tofa was among the Rajkumari's favourite beings. After Tofa fell sick and died in Shimla, news of the Rajkumari being upset reached Gandhi. He wrote to her saying, 'I hope you no longer grieve over Tofa's death... Don't have another pet animal if you can't restrain yourself.'[23] Her personal life was minimal beyond this. All the intensive running around she did was far removed from a life of luxury. The Rajkumari also wrote about one of her brothers being concerned for her: 'Shummy (Shamsher) would get very anxious about my health because of the hard work and the months of heat I had to endure for Bapu (Gandhi) and hence he (Bapu) would pack me off up to Simla (Shimla) every now and again to pacify Shummy.'[24]

To get out of the sweltering heat of the Sevagram Ashram, Kasturba Gandhi (Gandhi's wife) also travelled to Shimla and stayed at the Rajkumari's family home—a spacious bungalow named Manorville Mansion. Soon after Kasturba returned to Sevagram, the Rajkumari sent a box of apples from her family's orchard accompanied with a letter reaffirming her dedication to the ideals of serving people. She also sent raisins to Gandhi's ashram.[25]

---

[23]Gandhi, Mohandas, and Amrit Kaur, *Letters to Rajkumari Amrit Kaur*, Navajivan Publishing House, 1961.

[24]Ibid.

[25]'Gandhiji Frequented Shimla, Wasn't Fond of It', *The Tribune*, 28 September 2019, https://tinyurl.com/mvrb3p4m. Accessed on 23 June 2023.

Pine and deodar forests served as a backdrop to her bungalow which was modelled on the principles of Georgian architecture. Gandhi, who loathed Shimla because of its hand-pulled carts, often had to travel to the town as it was the 'summer capital' of the British Raj. He had to address public gatherings there. Whenever he visited, much like Kasturba, he stayed at the Rajkumari's residence.

∽

When India gained independence, the Rajkumari was already prepared to shoulder the responsibility of a brand-new nation. She was the only female minister in the country's first Cabinet and was the first health minister of independent India. There exists a picture of India's very first cabinet. Among the 20 men in the picture are Dr Rajendra Prasad, Dr B.R. Ambedkar and Jawaharlal Nehru. The lone woman among them is Rajkumari Amrit Kaur.[26]

Gandhi in his letter to the Rajkumari, dated August 1947, said: 'So you are minister. You have to be firm and true.'[27] His advice to her was to insist on teamwork as that way she would be kept abreast of things happening

---

[26]'HT Archives: The First Cabinet of Independent India Comes into Existence', *Hindustan Times*, 14 August 2017, https://tinyurl.com/2s3nvmu9. Accessed on 21 June 2023.

[27]Gandhi, Mohandas, and Amrit Kaur, *Letters to Rajkumari Amrit Kaur*, Navajivan Publishing House, 1961.

around her. Another letter refers to her position as the health minister. In that Gandhi said: 'Are you in charge of physical health only or moral also? The latter seems to be worse than the former.'[28]

The new Indian government had some tall challenges ahead of it. There were over 500 princely states at the time. The largest and richest states of Kashmir and Hyderabad were without peace. There was also the issue of rehousing refugees who had lost everything during Partition.

As the Rajkumari reached out to representatives of the international grant-provider, The Rockefeller Foundation, she had to redirect huge amounts of money meant for health reforms towards taking care of the refugees. They were, in her words, 'the victims of a national policy, of an undeclared war'.[29] Her department had spent ₹50 lakh per day on managing the Kashmir situation, and ₹12 lakh on the care of refugees who had fled from Pakistan.[30]

As the health minister, she had great plans to create a medical institution in Delhi. However, in the face of financial difficulties, it seemed as if these plans would never see the light of day. According to historian Sanjoy Bhattacharyya, while The Rockefeller Foundation had great confidence in the Rajkumari herself—referring to her as 'an intelligent, cultured woman' who would support

---

[28]Ibid.

[29]Bhattacharya, Sanjoy, *Expunging Variola: The Control and Eradication of Smallpox in India, 1947-1977*, Orient Longman, 2006.

[30]Ibid.

nursing as well as public health programmes—they had doubts about the new government's ability to bring out lasting reforms.[31]

A day before India ushered in a new age, at 11.00 p.m. the Constituent Assembly held a session with politician, freedom fighter and politician Sucheta Kripalani. Dr Rajendra Prasad addressed the gathering and Nehru made his famous 'Tryst with Destiny' speech in front of the Constituent Assembly. This gathering also included the Rajkumari.

During the formation of the new government of India, the Constituent Assembly was clear on making the country secular without any state religion, and this body advocated the freedom to practice all religions.

In a letter written in 1947 to Benegal B.N. Rau, one of the key members responsible for drafting India's Constitution, the Rajkumari mentioned: 'There are several customs practised in the name of religion eg; purdah, child marriage, polygamy, unequal laws of inheritance, prevention of inter-caste marriages, dedication of girls to temples (*devdasi*).'[32] The Constitution eventually said that the right to practice religion should not come in the way of enacting social reform.

On one hand, the fundamentals of a new nation were

---

[31]Ibid.

[32]Jha, Shefali, 'Rights versus Representation: Defending Minority Interests in the Constituent Assembly', *Economic and Political Weekly*, Vol. 38, No. 16, 19 April 2003.

being built brick by brick. But on the other, the events that had brought these leaders together became the cause of suffering for generations to come. Perhaps even the people in favour of India's partition had not estimated the scale of migration and violence that followed it. In Purana Qila itself there were more than 50,000 refugees that the Rajkumari went to check on.[33]

The Rajkumari would also keep Gandhi posted on the events in Punjab with regularity. 'The Punjab situation is bad beyond measure,' she wrote, recounting how a fellow Punjabi had spoken about how they had avenged the death of their murdered Punjabi brethren.[34]

The brutal loss of life under the mantle of avenging a community—any community—was not acceptable to her. She said, 'The tragedy is that most of us inwardly rejoice when our community gets its own back on the other... I am filled with fear as to where we are drifting.'[35]

She was right to fear. India has still not recovered from the wounds inflicted by Partition.

Sardar Vallabhbhai Patel and the Rajkumari also kept Gandhi posted on the violence that Delhi was witnessing. Gandhi wanted to go to Punjab but he was asked not to. Despite reports of all the violence, the Rajkumari visited

---

[33]Tan, Tai Yong, and Gyanesh Kudaisya, *The Aftermath of Partition in South Asia: Routledge Studies in the Modern History of Asia*, Routledge, 2002.
[34]Gandhi, Mohandas, and Amrit Kaur, *Letters to Rajkumari Amrit Kaur*, Navajivan Publishing House, 1961.
[35]Ibid.

the land of her ancestors. She returned with horrific stories. People had lost all their material possessions and homes; there was brutal violence; and they had no way of knowing whether their loved ones were safe. She later wrote that there was a 'complete lack of confidence on the part of minorities in the police administration both in East and West Punjab'.[36]

After a crude bomb exploded near Gandhi's prayer meeting, everyone was concerned about his welfare. On 28 January 1948, the Rajkumari asked if all was well during Gandhi's meeting that day. He assured her it was, going on to say: 'If I am to die by the bullet of a madman, I must do so smiling. There must be no anger within me. God must be in my heart and on my lips. And you promise me one thing. Should such a thing happen, you are not to shed one tear.'[37]

About 48 hours later, three crimson spots on his frail body marked his death. In the blink of an eye, Nathuram Godse's name forever became a part of India's history. He was, after all, the man who shot Gandhi.

When the flames were consuming Gandhi's mortal remains on 31 January 1948, the Rajkumari sat close by watching the pyre on the banks of the Yamuna River—

---

[36]Ibid.

[37]Aranha, Jovita, 'The 5 Attempts on Mahatma Gandhi's Life: Who, Why and When', *Citizens for Justice and Peace*, 31 January 2018, https://tinyurl.com/2p85cjrx. Accessed on 30 April 2023.

mourning with the leaders seated on the ground.[38] Gandhi was gone. But their work had to go on.

Even though working in a new government must have been a demanding task, the Rajkumari knew of the most immediate concerns India had as a new nation. One of these concerns was finding homes for the thousands of refugees in Jammu and Kashmir. Jawaharlal Nehru, in a letter to Vallabhbhai Patel, had mentioned how the then Maharaja of Kashmir was 'completely oblivious of this aspect or the international implications of the Kashmir issue'.[39]

Nehru went on to say that the Maharaja was behaving in a 'manner which is completely inexplicable to me and which irritates the people. There is at present a vitally urgent problem of arranging for the destitute refugees in Jammu—forty thousand or more.'[40]

There was also the fear of cholera and typhoid spreading through Jammu and Kashmir then. People from Rajkumari's health ministry had realized that the Maharaja's farm could temporarily be converted into a refugee camp and that his horses could be sent to Srinagar for a while. 'The Maharaja refused to permit this even though Amrit Kaur and Lady Mountbatten begged him for it. Meanwhile, children are dying in Jammu's streets,'

---

[38]Tan, Tai Yong, and Gyanesh Kudaisya, *The Aftermath of Partition in South Asia: Routledge Studies in the Modern History of Asia*, Routledge, 2002.
[39]Agrawal, Purushottam, *Who Is Bharat Mata? On History, Culture, and the Idea of India: Writings by and on Jawaharlal Nehru*, Speaking Tiger Publishing, 2019.
[40]Ibid.

wrote Nehru.[41] Even though the Rajkumari had given up so much in life, many from princely backgrounds equivalent to her own had learnt nothing from her sterling example.

The Rajkumari asked those who came from privileged backgrounds like hers to use their position to serve the country well. She urged them to emerge from their cocoons and come to the aid of their less-privileged brethren, underlining the importance of bridging the gap between the two classes.

In the words of independence activist Aruna Asaf Ali, 'Rajkumari Amrit belonged to a generation of pioneers. They belonged to well-to-do homes but gave up on their affluent and sheltered lives and flocked to Gandhiji's banner when he called women to join the national liberation struggle.'[42]

The Rajkumari was elected as the president of the World Health Assembly in 1950 and led the Indian delegation to the World Health Organization (WHO) for four years. She was not just the first woman to hold the post but was also the first Asian to do so. She also served as the chairperson of the Indian Red Cross and also started an association to fight tuberculosis in India and the Central Leprosy Teaching and Research Institute (CLTRI) in Chennai.[43]

---

[41]Ibid.

[42]*Eminent Parliamentarians Monograph Series*, Lok Sabha Secretariat, 1993.

[43]'Rajkumari Amrit Kaur, 75, Dies; India's First Minister of Health; Gandhi's Secretary 17 Years, a Princess, Led Campaign to Eradicate

Back in 1946, foreseeing the demands of a new country, the Rajkumari had also founded the Rajkumari Amrit Kaur College of Nursing (RAKCON) in Delhi. This was to ensure a steady supply of healthcare professionals that India would need. This act was a profound echo of her father's own involvement in the cause of educating and training women as health professionals.

In 1943, Sir Joseph William Bhore, an Indian civil servant, was tasked with doing a survey of health conditions and services in British India and had then had recommended a proposal to establish a national medical centre which would host qualified professionals.[44] This was the dream that Kaur shared with Bhore and even Nehru—a dream that she could not pursue due to limited resources.

When she found a chance, the Rajkumari piloted the Bill for this shared dream. Though the foundation stone was laid back in 1952, the institution was finally created in 1956. This was the All India Institute of Medical Sciences (AIIMS) in Delhi.

The Rajkumari was the first president of AIIMS—an institution that continues to be among India's best. Her appeals for aid were answered from across the globe. Monetary and material help came from Australia, Sweden,

---

Malaria', *The New York Times*, 7 February 1964, https://tinyurl.com/2fd42vzu. Accessed on 23 June 2023.

[44] *Report of the Health Survey and Development Committee Survey Vol. I*, The Manager of Publications, Delhi, 1945.

West Germany and the United States (US). New Zealand also donated £1 million towards the building of AIIMS. This just goes to show the personal goodwill that the Rajkumari had built up.[45]

All her contributions towards healthcare also got her an honorary degree from Princeton University in 1956. Her citation included the following words: 'A Princess in her nation's service. She has gone among the poor and the weak, the mothers and the children, the sick and the starving, not only with messages of hope and faith but also with substantial and highly effective programs of action.'[46] The Rajkumari was also associated with the launch of the Delhi Music Society in 1953. She left a mark in shaping the future of Indian sports too.

The first Asian Games was conceptualized in 1951. The invitations for this event were sent out in 1949. Delhi did not even have a proper stadium or track back then. Field Marshal K.M. Cariappa, first commander-in-chief of the Indian Army, loaned out defence buildings for temporary use while the Rajkumari personally chipped in to help finance India's future in sports. She did not always see eye-to-eye with the Field Marshal, but a shared

---

[45]Roychowdhury, Adrija, 'Rajkumari Amrit Kaur: The Princess Who Built AIIMS', *The Indian Express*, 26 August 2020, https://tinyurl.com/2p8yrt37. Accessed on 23 June 2023.

[46]'Rajkumari Amrit Kaur, 75, Dies; India's First Minister of Health; Gandhi's Secretary 17 Years, a Princess, Led Campaign to Eradicate Malaria', *The New York Times*, 7 February 1964, https://tinyurl.com/yn8febhb. Accessed on 30 April 2023.

love for sports smoothened their collaborations.

In 1953, Rajkumari Amrit organized coaching for sports for the first time in independent India. Understanding well enough the need for systematic routine to hone talent, she allocated money to establish a National Coaching Scheme. This further led to the establishment of the Netaji Subhas National Institute of Sports (NSNIS) in Patiala.

After she was elected the president of the All India Tennis Association (AITA) in 1954, she wrote to Field Marshal Cariappa lamenting how 'Like all other sports organizations, I found it [the Tennis Association] completely bankrupt and full of intrigue.'[47] In all likelihood, the Rajkumari must have done her best to clean up the department, and muscle it up for the sake of the sport she loved.

When Field Marshal Cariappa was India's ambassador to Australia in 1954, the Rajkumari requested him to send an Australian tennis coach to be employed at the NSNIS in Patiala. Since Australia had already established itself in the sport, she knew that they would surely have had good coaches.

Her concern was not just limited to the sport she pursued for much of her life. She also asked him to find a fast-bowling and a wicket-keeping coach for the cricket team, since we already had a slow-bowling all-rounder (Vinoo Mankad) and a fielding coach (C.K. Nayudu).

---

[47]Guha, Ramachandra, *India After Gandhi: The History of the World's Largest Democracy*, Picador, 2008.

In his book, Ramachandra Guha has mentioned that though Kaur's wishes could not come true at the time due to lack of foreign capital, they showcased her clarity of vision and knowledge of the field.

In 2014, when the Sherborne Girls' School (formerly Sherborne School for Girls) started sifting through their century-old archives in quest for inspirational women, they dug out the Rajkumari's name.

They recognized her contribution with these words: 'In a crumpled envelope in the archives we found the most incredible life. Amrit was one of Gandhi's companions and secretaries for many years, and was imprisoned three times by the British for pushing for (India's) independence.' They went on to acknowledge her as a 'pioneer, a woman of real presence and importance [...] an example to us all'.[48]

Her ancestral property, the beautiful Manorville in Shimla was donated to AIIMS to serve as a holiday home for the medical fraternity. The room in which Gandhi used to stay has been preserved as it was.

∽

The Rajkumari never married. She lived a life that witnessed the world going to war twice. She witnessed

---

[48]Magazine, Dorset, 'Sherborne Girls Celebrates the Extraordinary Lives of its Inspiring Alumni', *Great British Life*, 20 March 2014, https://tinyurl.com/s237ytye. Accessed on 30 April 2023.

the transition of India into an independent country with people who could make their own decisions. After a life filled with demanding roles that included being a freedom fighter; a Gandhian social reformer; a Parliamentarian; a sportsperson; a suffragette and more—the Rajkumari breathed her last in 1964 in New Delhi, a few months before Nehru's death. She was 75.

Holding onto the Bible and the Gita during tough times, she had on the iron *kadha*—a marker of her ancestral faith—when she was cremated along the banks of the Yamuna.

After a life spent working for others, the Rajkumari likely had friends everywhere—from ashram dwellers who had committed their whole lives to Gandhi, to prominent leaders of the Indian national movement and the suffragettes fighting a different war in London.

The next time you see people come out in large numbers under skies both dark and sunny in acts of protest and solidarity or someone use their privilege in the best possible way, think of Rajkumari Amrit, dear reader. Think of how she fought for a country where everyone could enjoy a game they love and for access to quality healthcare for every Indian. As someone who had it all, she was prepared to give it all up in pursuit of an equal, independent country.

Razia

The Princess Who Was Sultan

MEHRAULI, 1236

Shah Turkan, the concubine of the deceased Sultan Iltutmish, knew she had to do something to fix the situation at hand. Her son was away from the court of Delhi and there was growing unrest among people. Egging that restlessness was none other than her stepdaughter, Princess Razia.

To keep things under check till her son returned, Shah Turkan decided it was best to imprison Razia right away. She told herself that they could have her executed once her son was back in Delhi. This was in line with the many schemes she had plotted to ensure her son sat on the throne of Delhi.

As Shah Turkan was organizing men to have Razia

arrested, the Princess was making her way to what was among the first mosques ever built in North India—the Quwwat-ul-Islam Masjid in Mehrauli.[1] Built by Sultan Qutb-ud-din Aibak, Razia knew this could be the place where she found an audience since it was a Friday—a day of prayer. It's possible that Razia was aware that this would be the right time to garner support from the people, and to highlight how the current Sultan didn't seem to care about his people.

Along with this, Razia had another ace up her sleeve. Her chosen spot to garner support was only a few feet away from the spot where her father, Sultan Iltutmish, lay buried.

On the chosen Friday, Razia had everyone's attention even before she entered the mosque area. Along with the fact that women were not allowed inside mosques, it was also the sheer theatrics of how she made her entrance that made the event even more memorable. She was clad in red from head to toe. A lot of the retelling of this scene—from Shan Turkan preparing to imprison Razia and the latter preparing to stage a revolution—comes from the

[1]Salam, Ziya Us, 'There Was a Time When Muslim Women in India Not Only Prayed in Mosques, They Even Built Them', *Scroll.in*, 3 December 2019, https://tinyurl.com/bdd73hzb. Accessed on 26 June 2023.

journal *Indian Historical Quarterly* as well as historian Minhaj-i Siraj Juzjani's *Tabakat-i-Nasiri.*

When she had everyone's attention, Princess Razia reminded all those who had gathered around of her father's reign. This was not the kingdom her father had foreseen, she told them. She spoke of the current Sultan's thoughtlessness and all the atrocities they had to bear after he came to power. The current Sultan, she reminded them, should not have been chosen in the first place. That was her right as her father's chosen heir. Iltutmish, she said, had wanted her to be the next Sultan.[2]

The Princess had rallied enough support for herself by the time she finished her speech. People who had assembled there no longer accepted the current state of things. There would be a rebellion. And just like that, the tide turned in favour of the red-robed Princess. Here she was, hours away from being imprisoned by Shah Turkan, and she had managed to incite a rebellion. When the Sultan returned to Delhi, he expected to find Razia behind bars. Instead, it was his mother who waited for him in jail.

---

[2]Chandra, Satish, *Medieval India: From Sultanat to the Mughals Delhi Sultanat (1206-1526) Part-1*, Har Anand Publication, 2019.

RAZIA'S STORY

The Delhi Sultanate stayed in power for a little over three centuries. Their story begins when Qutb-ud-din Aibak, a general leading the armies of Muhammad of Ghor, came to North India. Parts of modern-day Afghanistan, Bangladesh and Iran were also part of his territories. Muhammad of Ghor had no biological children, and his generals became his successors, divvying up his lands after his death in 1206.

By 1206, Aibak had more or less emerged as the leader after winning over large territories. His hold was only strengthened by loyalists such as Shams ud-Din Iltutmish, who was the then governor of Budaun (in modern-day Uttar Pradesh).

The Delhi Sultanate comprised five successive Turko-Afghan dynasties—the Mamluk, Khilji, Tughlaq, Sayyid and the Lodi dynasties. Aibak was from the Mamluk dynasty, which took on 'slaves' who could wield immense power. According to historian John Keay, in this unusual line of kings, all the sultans were either former slaves or descendants of slaves. Mamluk is Arabic for 'owned', which is why the dynasty is also referred to as the 'Slave Dynasty'.[3]

Aibak's was a short reign. An accident following a nasty fall from his horse meant sudden death for the Sultan whose influence had spread as far as Bengal. He

[3]Husain, Mabdi, *The Rehla of Ibn Battuta,* Oriental Institute Baroda, 1976.

had not nominated his successor and, in light of this, Aram Shah (whom some presume to be his son) took over. Aram Shah did not have popular support. Even the Turkish court, which had a strong say in matters of the Delhi Sultanate, looked favourably on Iltutmish, who had served Aibak faithfully.

Iltutmish had a bittersweet childhood. According to the Persian historian Minhaj-i Siraj Juzjani, his father loved him so much that his older brothers began to hate him. It was out of this envy that they made a plan to trick him. The brothers convinced Iltutmish to accompany them to a horse show. The trip was a ruse to get him away from his family. At the very first opportunity, Iltutmish was sold off to a slave trader. He was not even a teenager when all of this happened.

Under the guidance of the Qazi of Bukhara, Iltutmish received a liberal education. According to Minhaj, at one point of time, Iltutmish lost some money in the market when he was sent out to get grapes.

While worrying about how his master would react, Iltutmish met a wandering *fakir*. The holy man said to Iltutmish, 'Stop crying, you were not meant to weep.'[4] The fakir bought him grapes and then pronounced that one day he'd attain power and wealth. The fakir then told him that he should always care for the ascetics and *darwesh*, much like one of them had taken care of him.

[4]Juzjani, Minhaj-i-Siraj, *Tabakat-i-Nasiri, Vol. I*, H.G. Raverty (trans.), Digital Library of India, 1881.

This dream of having power one day in the future might have had a strange effect on the boy, especially since his life took one strange turn after another. The Qazi who had taken the boy under his protection died, and he was again sold off to another master. This time, he was taken to Baghdad, which was, at the time, known to be a great spiritual centre. Here too, somehow, Iltutmish was largely at the receiving end of blessings.

Having been born into a well-off family, and later having spent time among learned people, perhaps it was easy for him to win reverence as he progressed into adulthood. Some writers, like Rafiq Zakaria, describe him as a man of unusual vigour, and many highlight the parallels between Iltutmish's story and that of Joseph from the Bible—the latter too is sold off by his brothers but grows in prominence at a court faraway.

The experiences that shaped Iltutmish's life, one assumes, must have made him a sensible leader. Perhaps Aibak saw these leadership skills in him early on. It's also possible that Aibak thought of Iltutmish as his own son. Besides, his administrative experience made him an ideal candidate for leading Delhi. When invited to Delhi, the nobles at the court earnestly welcomed him. He was even married to Aibak's daughter to strengthen his claim to the throne.[5]

---

[5]Bhushan, Jamila Brij, *Sultan Raziya, Her Life and Times: A Reappraisal*, Manohar Publications, 1990.

When the news of Iltutmish's elevation reached Aram Shah, he challenged him for Aibak's throne. But Iltutmish defeated his unpopular rival with ease. Aram Shah managed to escape the battlefield, and Iltutmish was formally crowned as the Sultan in 1211. He was the one who moved the royal court to Delhi from Lahore, becoming the founder of the Delhi Sultanate.[6]

Iltutmish's reign was difficult. Along with the Turk nobles who expected to have influence in his court, he also had to fend off a Mongol invasion at the behest of the infamous Genghis Khan. This meant going to war with the neighbouring Rajput kingdoms. He won one fort, one kingdom after another, including Ranthambore, on his march to expansion.

Iltutmish's eldest son was Nasir-ud-din Mahmud. Muiz-ud-din Bahram and Rukn-ud-din Firoz were two of his other sons. His eldest daughter, born in 1205, was Razia.

She was about six when her father established himself in Mehrauli, Delhi. She was old enough to see her father attend court and carry on the work Aibak had begun—of building monuments that time could not erase. Aibak had built one storey of the famed Qutub Minar. Iltutmish added another three storeys to it. He is also credited with building the walls and gates that surround the Minar.[7]

---

[6]Smith, R.V., 'Diadems of Death', *The Hindu*, 8 November 2010, https://tinyurl.com/5n6nz9r8. Accessed on 25 June 2023.

7 'Haunting Legacy', *Frontline*, 4 January 2017, https://tinyurl.com/bd9262tb. Accessed on 26 June 2023.

Iltutmish treated Razia no differently from his sons. He insisted that Razia be given the same formal training in arms, administration, diplomacy and horsemanship that her eldest brother Nasir did. Nasir could easily have been the most eligible claimant to his father's throne but that was not to be.

It's likely that Iltutmish was observant enough to notice the ways of the court. Razia always had a say in things, much to the surprise of many who felt that a woman should only be seen and not heard.

The fact that her father held her opinions in high regard is made apparent from the time he left Delhi to go and visit Gwalior for some work in 1231. Razia was given the reins of his court then.

Since it was considered inappropriate for Muslim women to be seen without a veil, Razia kept her veil on. She was mostly mindful of social precedents at the time and displayed grace while she exercised royal authority in her father's name. A brief taste of power did not go to her head—something that contrasts with the behaviour some of her family members displayed.

The Sultan was so happy with how Razia had handled things in his absence that when he returned to Delhi, he had his minister (Taj-ul-Mulk Mahmud) draw up a document stating that she would be his successor. When questioned about why he was naming a woman as his heir apparent, Iltutmish is believed to have said, 'My sons are devoted to the pleasures of youth and not one of them is qualified to be king. After my death, it will be seen that there is no one more competent to guide the state than my daughter.'[8]

It is perhaps because Aibak had not named a successor before his death that Iltutmish realized the importance of doing so. The throne had not come easily to him. He literally had to fight for it. Thus, naming Razia as his successor points towards his hope of his children getting the throne.

Iltutmish's eldest son, Nasir, died in 1228. Had he still been alive, Iltutmish would have had to choose between him and Razia. Nasir had already proved himself as the governor of Awadh and Bengal. Had Nasir still been in the picture, perhaps there would have been no other considerations. But sometimes things happen despite great odds. The Sultan knew that naming Razia as his heir was contentious, but he still went ahead with the decision.

After a brief illness in 1236, Iltutmish passed away as well. After his death, the nobles decided his will could easily be disregarded. They proceeded to choose another one of Iltutmish's children—a son—to sit on his throne.

As mentioned earlier, Shah Turkan saw this as the perfect opportunity to have the nobles name her own son as the new king. She found this to be particularly easy, considering the nobles were wary of having a female

---

[8]Eraly, Abraham, *The Age of Wrath: A History of the Delhi Sultanate*, Viking, 2014.

ruler. Acting swiftly, she had Rukn-ud-din Firoz appointed as the new Sultan.

It was not a matter of leadership qualities or talent. This was an issue of gender alone. Though chosen by her father as his successor, in the eyes of the court, Razia was not the right person to rule solely because of her gender. The nobles later found out that they were heavily misguided in their decision.

One can admire the great irony of placing Rukn-ud-din Firoz on the throne. The only reason he was chosen was because the nobles did not want to answer to a woman. But in a way, that is exactly what happened. Shah Turkan began to take undue advantage of her new-found power and rained abuses down on the very people who had helped her son get the throne.

Even with all the power she wielded, Shah Turkan was insecure about her position. Her desire to destroy the chances of Razia succeeding was so strong that she kept plotting and hatching conspiracies.

Razia was not the only one who suffered the consequences of Shah Turkan's actions. Several other people had been tortured and killed by her. For instance, another one of Iltutmish's sons was blinded and killed. He was a young boy but Shah Turkan just saw a threat to her own son's crown.

This single-minded chase for power had its repercussions. All the influence Shah Turkan had built up and all the alliances she had made began to fade.

It's likely that people began to resent her and her son as well. There was a mistrust for the new government because it looked like the new Sultan seemed to be more interested in chasing material pleasures, and squandering money than looking after the Sultanate's affairs.

According to Minhaj, Rukn-ud-din Firoz was handsome and generous. But he was also addicted to merrymaking and spent everything he could on having a good time. 'No King in any reign had ever scattered gifts, robes of honor, and grants in the way he did,' writes Minhaj. He goes on to describe how the King would ride out drunk on an elephant, commanding it to go through bazaars and streets, throwing *tankas* (coins) of red gold for people to pick up.[9]

It was not long before his disrespectful ways and disregard for courtly affairs led to his courtiers and citizens publicly expressing their displeasure. According to historian Jamila, small rebellions started breaking out throughout their territories. His own nobles, including his wazir, abandoned him. Enraged by the turn of events, Rukn-ud-din Firoz marched out of Delhi to deal with the rebels. Allegedly his own troops joined the enemy and killed his attendants.

Taking note of the shifting winds, Razia is likely to have realized how fragile her stepmother's influence

---

[9]Juzjani, Minhaj-i-Siraj, *Tabakat-i-Nasiri, Vol. I,* H.G. Raverty (trans.), Digital Library of India, 1881.

and her stepbrother's powers were. She waited for the right time to claim what was rightfully hers, and set off to the Quwwat-ul-Islam Masjid in Mehrauli to kindle the fire of discontent. As mentioned earlier, her speech was a rousing success.

Once Rukn-ud-din was back in Delhi, he was imprisoned and executed soon after. His unsteady reign of the Delhi Sultanate lasted for only six months and 28 days.[10]

When the nobles were looking for someone to shoulder the heavy burden of being the next Sultan, Razia is believed to have waved her scarf from the window and said,

> Here I am, the daughter of His Majesty; the crown befits my head. It was I who was chosen as his heir-apparent. Since you set the crown on another's head against the king's orders, you've had to grieve. Give me the crown, and should I prove to be a better ruler than a man, keep me on the throne. Else remove the crown from my head and give it to someone else.[11]

As written by the historian A.B.M. Habibullah, 'In the thirteenth and fourteenth centuries the idea of a woman

---

[10]Bhushan, Jamila Brij, *Sultan Raziya, Her Life and Times: A Reappraisal*, Manohar Publications, 1990.

[11]Eraly, Abraham, *The Age of Wrath: A History of the Delhi Sultanate*, Viking, 2014.

ruler was no more repugnant to Islamic law.'[12] There were Turkish Sultans who were still legally slaves and there were kings with physical challenges, but it was still difficult for most to accept a female Sultan. The reason for objection to Razia's ascension was a psychological one alone. Women of Persian nobility commanded respect and influenced politics, yes, but to see a woman hold all that power was unsettling for many.

Abdul Malik Isami, a fourteenth-century poet and historian, notes that the nobles got together and agreed that 'a daughter is better than an ill-bred son. Many a woman has been the vanquisher of men in battle; many a man has owed his position to a woman.'[13] And so, like it was meant to be, Razia was invited to take the throne. According to Archana Garodia Gupta's book, in November 1236 Razia was given the title of 'Jalalat-ud-din'. She was now the Sultan.

∽

It was clear that Razia's belief in the power of learning and knowledge was immense. It was during her time that the Madarasa-i-Nasiriya was elevated as a centre for

[12]Gabbay, Alyssa, 'In Reality a Man: Sultan Iltutmish, His Daughter, Raziya, and Gender Ambiguity in Thirteenth Century Northern India', *Journal of Persianate Studies*, Vol. 4, No. 1, 2011, pp. 45–63.

[13]Eraly, Abraham, *The Age of Wrath: A History of the Delhi Sultanate*, Viking, 2014.

learning.[14] In fact, it was Razia who brought the historian Minhaj to Delhi. As someone who came from a family of scholars and had a head for administration, Minhaj saw Razia's method of working and documented it. She was a known patron of learning centres and *khanqahs* (places for Sufi saints).

Minhaj writes that Razia was focussed on reorganizing administration. As written by him: 'The kingdom became pacified, and the power of the state was greatly extended. From the territories of Lakhnauti (Gauda, now on the border of India and Bangladesh) to Debal (ancient port near modern-day Karachi) all the *maliks* and *amirs* manifested their obedience and submission.'[15]

Noting how turbulent things had been in Delhi, the Sultanate's governors had been dissenting against the Crown. But Razia was able to quell the rebellions and get things under control, a fact that didn't go unnoticed by the court. Now people had finally begun to see her for her true capabilities, and not just as someone who was the better option than their previous Sultan.

For close to three years, Razia had a good handle on things. There were those, of course, who continued to resent her. However, even they could not fault her for

---

[14]Jahan, Farhat, *Depiction of Women in the Sources of the Delhi Sultanate, (1206–1388)*, Centre of Advanced Study, Department of History, Aligarh Muslim University, 2012.

[15]Juzjani, Minhaj-i-Siraj, *Tabakat-i-Nasiri, Vol. I*, H.G. Raverty (trans.), Digital Library of India, 1881.

much. They never stopped looking for a reason though. They finally found their reason when Razia began to appear in public in a manner deemed unsuitable for Muslim women.

She switched her dresses and veils for tunics and caps. She was seen walking around with a bow and quiver. Most scandalous of all was that she had discarded her veil. She rode out on elephants without a veil, and her courtiers followed her on horseback. According to people, Razia exercising her right to choose how to dress was unacceptable. Nobles who disliked her used this to convince orthodox Muslims that Razia was unfit for her role.[16]

To see their Sultan, a woman, riding about on an elephant without a veil may have displeased some, but during her reign, there was peace in Delhi (even when wars due to internal politics carried on outside). There is the case of Muhammad Junaidi, for instance. Formerly, a wazir of the kingdom, Junaidi was a powerful man who had openly opposed Razia's ascension to the throne. When Shah Turkan was working to put her son on the throne, she did so with Junaidi's support. When Razia became the ruler, she crushed his rebellion. At another time when Delhi was under threat from insurgents, Razia chose to go in the field and not send her commanders

---

[16]Jahan, Farhat, *Women in Delhi Sultanate (1206–1388 AD)*, LAP Lambert Academic Publishing, 2013.

in her stead. She set up her tents by the Yamuna, fearless in the face of mortal danger.[17]

When the Delhi Sultanate established itself in India, it also brought along many of the customs followed in central and west Asia. One of these was that the *khutba* (the sermon during Friday prayers at a mosque), was read in the name of the person who was the head of the Islamic community at large. If the khutba was read in a particular ruler's name, it signified their acceptance and reinforced their status as a ruler. In one of North India's first mosques, Quwwat-ul-Islam, the khutba was read in Razia's name.[18]

Razia is known to have established schools and public libraries. Philosophy, astronomy and other sciences flourished in these schools. Historian Shahana Dasgupta, describes Razia as the 'People's Queen'.[19] This is because she repaired roads and set up fortifications to discourage dacoits. She met with craftspeople and farmers, travelling extensively in her territories.

Razia's accomplishments after she came to power were considerable, but her rivals and select courtiers

[17]Chatterjee, Anjali, 'Role of Women in the Politics of Early Delhi Sultanate—A Case Study of Shah Turkan', *Proceedings of the Indian History Congress*, Vol. 59, 1998, pp. 404–6.

[18]Salam, Ziya Us, 'There Was a Time When Muslim Women in India Not Only Prayed in Mosques, They Even Built Them', *Scroll.in*, 3 December 2019, https://tinyurl.com/bdd73hzb. Accessed on 26 June 2023.

[19]Dasgupta, Shahana, *Razia: The People's Queen*, Rupa Publications, 2001.

could never accept her being in power. They resented the hold she had. She dressed like a man, went out in public without a veil, rode horses and called herself 'Sultan' instead of 'Sultana'. The term 'Sultana', as mentioned by historian Shahana Dasgupta, indicated to Razia that she was a Sultan's consort (rather than the Sultan herself).[20] She was not the consort of a dead Sultan. She was not the mother of a young prince on whose behalf she was ruling. She was Delhi's first female ruler in her own right. That is where her personal disapproval of the title 'Sultana' came from.

A parallel can be drawn here with Queen Elizabeth I. While addressing troops assembled (before they went on to ward off a Spanish invasion) at Tilbury Camp in Essex, in August 1588, the Queen famously remarked, 'I know I have the body but of a weak and feeble woman; but I have the heart and stomach of a king, and of a King of England too.'[21]

Another parallel could be Rudrama Devi from Orugallu (presently Warangal in Telangana). In the records of Marco Polo (a Venetian traveller and merchant), who was in India in the thirteenth century, there is mention of an independent queen—Rudrama Devi.[22] He sang high praises for her way of administration and called her 'a

---

[20]Ibid.

[21]Marcus, Leah S., Janel Mueller and Mary Beth Rose, *Elizabeth I: Collected Works,* The University of Chicago Press, 2002.

[22]Yule, Henry, *The Travels of Marco Polo,* Outlook Verlag, 2018.

lover of justice, of equity, and of peace'. But he made an error in his accounts; he assumed Rudrama Devi was a widow who had inherited her dead husband's kingdom.

Rudrama Devi was actually the only child of Ganapati Deva, the ruler of the Kakatiya Dynasty. On the advice of his prime minister, the King had a ceremony to mark Rudrama Devi as his successor. But unlike Razia, Rudrama came into power during her early teens and ruled alongside her father. After a series of losses to a rival, Ganapati Deva retired from public life and Rudrama ruled on her own. Like Razia, this sovereign also donned male garments.[23]

She went on to rule for a good 40 years—a striking contrast to how long Razia's rule would last.

It is popularly believed that Razia Sultan wanted to put an end to the *jizya*, a special tax that non-Muslims were required to pay. One can't be too certain if all her moves were purely political, but perhaps she was influenced by her father's legacy. Iltutmish is believed to have told his nobles that Muslims were as scarce in India as salt is in food, so the leaders should not antagonize the Hindus.[24]

---

[23]Deshpande, Abhinay, 'Rare Sculpture of Rudrama Devi's "Last" Battle Discovered', *The Hindu*, 8 April 2018, https://tinyurl.com/yhs3c8mb. Accessed on 26 June 2023.

[24]Kumar, Seshadri, 'India Should Be Grateful to Alauddin Khilji for Thwarting the Mongol Invasions', *The Wire*, 9 December 2017, https://tinyurl.com/4khvmaub. Accessed on 30 April 2023.

Regardless of what Iltutmish had said, Razia's courtiers were likely taken aback at her proposing to remove the tax. They justified the tax by saying that it helped finance the royal court, while also establishing the superiority of the Muslim state. According to Minhaj, the nobles argued that by paying this tax the Hindus were not required to fight for the Sultan, so it was a fair transaction.

One assumes that Razia wanted Hindus and Muslims to be treated equally, as that way both factions would loyal to their Sultan. Much to the wrath of many, Razia managed to have this tax abolished. Changes like this are never easily accepted anywhere. And this was only one of the few things that Razia wanted to amend.

Sultan Aibak had initially appointed a group of 40 nobles—known as the Corps of Forty, Dal Chalisa or the Amir-i-Chahalgani—to assist him in administration. Iltutmish had somewhat modified this group but it was still essentially a group that commanded great influence in the Delhi Sultanate. Though the Sultan commanded power entirely, this appointed circle of people helped in exercising that power.[25]

This Corps of Forty was shocked when Razia appointed people outside their circle as officers of the court. One such person was Jamal-ud-din Yaqut, an Abyssinian (Ethiopian) slave.

---

[25]Pillai, Manu S., 'Women on the Throne: From Indira to Raziya', *mint*, 4 November 2016, https://tinyurl.com/272ctkpb. Accessed on 26 June 2023.

Historian A.B.M. Habibullah believes that Razia was well aware of the danger presented by her father's Turkish officers and slaves.[26] They were the ones who wielded power in the state. But it is likely that they saw an outsider like Yaqut's appointment as a threat to their power. It was necessary to follow this action by restoring the monarchy to its rightful position, as a dynastic leadership could yield results only when it commanded absolute power. In thirteenth-century India, the monarch's firmness was equivalent to their power. Courage and unflinching determination were Razia's motto. In strength of character, she proved herself equal to a man.

There is little evidence of Razia actually wanting to create a circle of people of her own, but the appointment of Yaqut was enough to get people talking.[27]

Razia had him appointed as the caretaker of her horse stables—a high honour and office. One cannot be too certain of their relationship, but it is insinuated that Razia was romantically involved with Yaqut. He could have been a confidante or an adviser, and not necessarily her lover. But this companionship was thoroughly looked down upon, perhaps owing to Yaqut's non-Turkish ancestry.

If Razia had been a man, this relationship would not

---

[26]Habibullah, A.B.M., 'Sulṭānah Rāziah', *The Indian Historical Quarterly*, Vol. 16, No. 1, 1940.

[27]Adhikari, Shona, 'Razia Sultan: The First Empress of India and the Confusion over Her Burial Site', *The Asian Age*, 8 August 2019, https://tinyurl.com/4nx8fj4z. Accessed on 25 June 2023.

have caused such a political storm. But rules worked differently for a woman, even then. Razia's private affairs were somehow everyone's business.

∽

Her companionship with Yaqut and her approach to making the court more inclusive, combined with her disdain for the purdah, was enough to bind her orthodox enemies together. But they knew well enough that she commanded support in Delhi, so any plans of sabotaging her would have to be executed elsewhere.

According to historian Satish Chandra, the first of the rebellions that started the end of Razia's time took place in Lahore. She marched to Lahore and succeeded in getting the governor, Kabir Khan, to submit to her. After handling this, she returned to Delhi only to get news that there was fresh trouble brewing in Taber-e-Hind (presently Bhatinda). Razia is likely to have reacted differently to news of this particular rebellion—after all, this was a little more personal. Tabar-e-Hind was governed by her childhood friend, Malik Altunia.[28]

She rode out to this part of Punjab immediately. What she did not know was that Altunia had joined forces with the nobles who opposed her, including her half-brother Muiz-ud-din Bahram. The rebellion was but a way to get

---

[28]Ibid.

her away so that she would not have home advantage. As Razia still had support in Delhi, the only way of ensuring she had no help was to trap her outside Delhi.

Overthrowing Razia had to be a two-pronged plan, and both parts had to be carried out simultaneously. While one band of her enemies killed Razia's loyalist Yaqut and imprisoned her at Tabarhinda (modern-day Bhatinda Fort), another band carried out a coup in Razia's court. In her absence, Bahram was elevated to the throne of Delhi in April 1240.

When viewed in retrospect, historical events seem repetitive—like a movie stuck in loop where only the actors are different. Razia had seized the throne when the previous Sultan was away, and now the same was being done to her.

∽

The next we hear of Razia is when she got married to Altunia, the man who had imprisoned her in Bhatinda Fort. It is unclear how this event shaped up. Perhaps this was an outcome of their childhood friendship; it is possible that agreeing to Altunia's marriage proposal might have been Razia's way of bargaining for freedom. It's also possible that Altunia's intention of marrying Razia was his attempt at paving a legitimate line to claim the throne of Delhi. Either way, both got what they wanted at that moment.

After their marriage, the two gathered their supplies and drummed up support to march towards Delhi sometime in late 1240. Historian John Keay writes that if the conduct of the army had been left up to Razia, the army was likely to have prevailed. But 'as a wife, she deferred to her husband and they were heavily defeated'.[29]

There are many different versions of what happened next. Some say their captors killed them there; some believe a band of thieves killed them later. Some also believe that the two were taken to the new Sultan who had them killed. The identity of the killer (or killers) remains unclear but Razia's death was final. She was only 35 when she died.[30]

∽

Razia's predecessor, her half-brother, spent about six months on the throne. Her successor, another half-brother, ruled for two years. Razia's reign lasted for about three years.[31]

Satish Chandra refers to her as a 'romantic figure in medieval history'. He goes on to say, 'Razia's firmness, and desire to exercise power directly was the major cause

---

[29]Keay, John, *India: A History*, Harper Press, 2010.
[30]Parihar, Rohit, 'Unwritten Epitaph', *India Today*, 3 August 2009, https://tinyurl.com/53n5mb7v. Accessed on 26 June 2023.
[31]Adhikari, Shona, 'Razia Sultan: The First Empress of India and the Confusion over Her Burial Site', *The Asian Age*, 8 August 2019, https://tinyurl.com/4nx8fj4z. Accessed on 25 June 2023.

of the dissatisfaction of the Turkish nobles.'[32]

Romanticizing her work, struggles and time doesn't quite do justice to the woman who ruled Delhi. In *Tabaqat-i-Nasiri*, Minhaj writes:

> Sultan Razia was a great monarch. She was wise, just and generous, a benefactor to the kingdom, a dispenser of justice, a protector for her subjects, and the leader of her armies. She was endowed with all qualities befitting a king, but she was not born of the right sex, and so in the estimation of men all these virtues were worthless.[33]

This disheartening note, sums up much in the history of women.

To some, like the historian Abdul Malik Isami, Razia's elevated position was so preposterous that he declared that a woman's place was at the spinning wheel and that the high office would only topple her sanity. According to what he wrote in 1350, Razia should have just made 'cotton her companion and grief her wine-cup'.[34]

It is necessary to reflect on how history is written and owned by victors and survivors. The historian Isami, mentioned previously, was an employee of Razia's successor.

---

[32]Chandra, Satish, *Medieval India: From Sultanat to the Mughals-Mughal Empire (1526–1748)*, Har Anand Publications, 2007.
[33]Juzjani, Minhaj-i-Siraj, *Tabaqat-i-Nasiri, Vol. I*, H.G. Raverty (trans.), Digital Library of India, 1881.
[34]Eraly, Abraham, *The Age of Wrath: A History of the Delhi Sultanate*, Viking, 2014.

Perhaps it was owing to his loyalty to the Razia's successor or plain hatred for what Razia represented, that caused the historian to write with such venom.

Isami also wrote about how the nobles at the court were 'scandalized' by Razia's actions. He further said:

> I am told she came out of her *purdah* suddenly, discarded her modesty and became jovial...she put on a male attire and cap...she mounted an elephant and went about publicly...she continued to hold a public durbar...everyone high and low used to enjoy the sight of her face...she began to ride escorted by state officers. This continued on for a full six months, everybody from lowest to highest became suspicious of her.[35]

Strange are the definitions of a 'scandal', morphing into different things depending on geography and time.

Scholar and documentarian Amir Khusrau, in his retelling of Razia's tale, wrote about the end of her fortunes:

> For three years in which her hand was strong,
> No one lay a finger on one of her orders.
> In the fourth, since the page had turned from her matters
> The pen of fate drew a line through her.[36]

[35] Haeri, Shahla, *The Unforgettable Queens of Islam: Succession, Authority, Gender*, Cambridge University Press, 2020.

[36] Gabbay, Alyssa, 'In Reality a Man: Sultan Iltutmish, His Daughter,

As Raza Rumi notes in his book *Delhi by Heart: Impressions of a Pakistani Traveller*, much of Delhi's past was defined by men. According to him, barring a few exceptions, this past is essentially made up of 'powerful and quarrelsome men vying for power and patronage'.[37]

Razia was a woman who stood against societal conventions. She was someone who kept up the fight against the patriarchy, by taking ownership of not just how she dressed and appeared in public but also of her name. She was not 'Sultana'. She was 'Sultan'. Irrespective of where she found her spirit, history needs to treat her better.

So large is the gap in piecing together Razia's story that even the location of her final resting place is debated. Some say that after her death, her half-brother Bahram took her back with him and buried her in Delhi. A popular version, documented by Abdul Malik Isami says that Razia and Altunia escaped the battlefield but crossed paths with a band of thieves who killed them in Kaithal in Haryana.

The Moroccan traveller, Ibn Battuta, paints an even more dramatic picture. He writes that after Razia's forces were defeated, she wandered off and came upon a farmer's field. She was so exhausted and hungry that

---

Raziya, and Gender Ambiguity in Thirteenth Century Northern India', *Journal of Persianate Studies,* Vol. 4, No. 1, 2011, pp. 45–63.

[37]Rumi, Raza, *Delhi by Heart: Impressions of a Pakistani Traveller*, Harper Collins, 2013.

she fell there. The farmer offered her a piece of bread. He didn't recognize who the woman in front of him was. But he did see jewels sewn into the embroidery of her garments. So, taking advantage of her state, he must have killed and buried her there for the jewels. Then the story mentions that he took the jewels with him to the market. But the local authorities grew suspicious and accused him of theft. He confessed to murder when they started beating him. [38]

Some, like Ibn Battuta, believe that the Sultan is buried in Kaithal. He writes that 'a small shrine was erected over her grave, which is visited by pilgrims and is considered a place of sanctity. It is situated on the banks of the Jumna.'[39]

There are also others who believe that descriptions of historians of those times are misinterpreted and that Razia Sultan is actually buried in Tonk, Rajasthan. Encased by hills on all sides, this place was once used by Iltutmish when he captured Ranthambore. The populace has for generations believed that Razia lies in the tomb there, because of the octagonal carving on the tomb stone that was typical of the Delhi Sultanate period.

The most popular supposition about her burial place is near the Bulbuli Khana Chowk in old Delhi's Turkman Gate area. This place has the support of the Archaeological

---

[38]Husain, Mabdi, *The Rehla of Ibn Battuta,* Oriental Institute Baroda, 1976.
[39]Ibid.

Survey of India, the keeper of the country's monuments.[40]

In the possibility that this really is Razia Sultan's grave, no one is very sure who occupies the grave next to her. Some believe it to be her sister; some say it's Altunia.

It is a wretched shame that Razia's final resting spot remains a thing of such conundrum. Additionally, these places lie enveloped in neglect. Her father is buried in the Qutub Minar complex in Mehrauli in a marble tomb with ornate carvings. This is a tomb fit for a Sultan of the Delhi Sultanate. What Razia Sultan has been given is plain brick and mortar, if that is even really her grave.

If you find yourself walking the bustling and serpentine labyrinth of lanes of Old Delhi, dear reader, look for the place where Razia lies buried. Her grave is one of the two near the small mosque, where the faithful gather to offer prayers. Decrepit buildings surround the place that lies marked as her grave. It makes for a rather dishonourable tribute to a Sultan of the Delhi Sultanate.

---

[40]Parihar, Rohit, 'Unwritten Epitaph', *India Today*, 3 August 2009, https://tinyurl.com/53n5mb7v. Accessed on 26 June 2023.

Nur

The Refugee Who Became an Empress

MATHURA, 1619

The air was electric with excitement and anticipation in the temple town of Mathura. Tales of something new happening had spread through the town, and fantastical stories dominated conversations. Some said they had seen painted elephants far away. Others quickly added that the elephants were nearby, and soon all the town folk would see them.

Runners who moved ahead of the royal party to announce their arrival had already reached the town. They played their drums and notified the people gathered that Mathura would soon be in the presence of royalty.

This was a time when Mughal emperors ruled over large tracts of India. Anytime they travelled, often after careful consideration of the most auspicious time to travel, they were accompanied by thousands of people. The grand master of the royal household would move ahead of the caravan, anticipating and deciding where to next set up a base for his King. He would set up tents and ensure that everything was in place before the royals arrived.

Soon enough, the hooves of horses trotting kicked up a cloud of dust that signalled that the wait was finally over. Splendid tents dotted the city's skyline and the Mughal emperor Nur-ud-din Muhammad Salim, better known as Jahangir, settled into the biggest of tents as custom dictated.

A group of local residents had been waiting to have an audience with Jahangir. It was a matter of life and death for anyone who lived in Mathura. The matter which weighed so heavily on their minds was relevant even for those just passing through the town. Deep in the dense forests that enveloped this place of pilgrimage, there walked a man-eating tiger who had evaded every trap set for it.

The local residents had gathered to ask Jahangir to save the city from the tiger. Jahangir's love for hunting tigers and lions was well known. Such was his fondness for hunting that he is said to have once spent three months doing so.

But a lot of time had passed since Jahangir had last gone hunting. When approached by the people in Mathura, he was perplexed because he had only recently renewed his vow of not harming a living being with his hands. This vow was taken for the sake of a grandchild who was unwell.

Jahangir then called upon the one person he knew for sure was as able a marksman as he was—Nur Jahan. There were many stories of Nur Jahan's skill as a hunter. Only a few years before the Mathura incident, the legendary Nur Jahan is said to have killed four tigers with six bullets.

The next day, even as the cold winds of October spread across Mathura, Nur Jahan and Jahangir rode towards the forest on their decorated elephants. Some of their courtiers followed in palanquins with silken sheets; others rode along on handsome horses. Then began their wait for the tiger that they had heard so much about.

They waited for hours, but the tiger did not appear. Then, as if seized by an invisible force, Nur Jahan and Jahangir's elephants began to sway from side to side. A less-seasoned person would have wondered why these large mammals were overcome by restlessness suddenly and disregarded their mahout's instructions. But as skilled hunters, Jahangir and Nur Jahan understood what this behaviour meant. According to historians like Ellison Banks Findly, it is believed that while being invisible to human eyes, the elephants had picked up on the tiger's presence.

In the book *The Jahangirnama: Memoirs of Jahangir, Emperor of India,* it can be seen that Jahangir had noted how an elephant can smell a tiger's presence and becomes restless (swaying from side to side). And if one is seated on an elephant at this time, it can be extremely difficult to fire a shot. But being on an elephant's back also gave some measure of safety. Now it was all up to Nur Jahan. If she attempted to shoot the tiger still hidden from their eyes, she would have to ensure that her aim was perfect.

People who saw the incident went on to say that Nur Jahan brought the tiger down in one shot. Jahangir's courtiers were somewhat familiar with Nur Jahan's aim, but the people who lived in the area went on to talk about the incident for days together. Such expertise with a gun was rare. What was rarer still was seeing a woman get acknowledged for her talents.

NUR JAHAN'S STORY

Picture Kandahar in the late 1500s. It was a time when caravans loaded with traders and families would traverse through open, inhospitable lands for a better future. It was a time of political persecution, and among those affected by the political turmoil were Mirza Ghiyas Beg and his wife Asmat Begum. Mirza Beg's father, a learned man of noble blood, was the prime minister to the Persian royal family.

The couple had three children. They realized that for the safety and betterment of their family, they had to leave Iran and start anew. They only had two mules to share as they made their way to greener pastures.

Despite a cloud of misfortune that came down upon them, this family went on to be deeply involved in royal affairs everywhere they went. For instance, the couple were grandparents to Mumtaz Mahal (in whose memory Shah Jahan built one of the seven wonders of the world—the Taj Mahal).[1]

To flee persecution in their native land after his father passed away, Mirza Beg and his wife set out on a journey via Kandahar and Lahore to Akbar's court in Fatehpur Sikri. They were forced to halt in Kandahar because the heavily pregnant Asmat Begum was about to have her fourth child.

---

[1]Faruqui, Munis D., *The Princes of the Mughal Empire, 1504-1719*, Cambridge University Press, 2012.

Though well off at one point of time, the couple's finances were in dire straits at the time of the journey. As if having to flee their home with the minimal things they could carry was not enough, their caravan was also attacked by a band of robbers who stole their possessions. And now they even had a child—a baby girl. She was but another mouth to feed when they were so down on their luck.

There are even some stories about how the couple left the child on the side of the road. Maybe they hoped that some kind-hearted person would take in the child. They had not travelled very far off when they were overcome by regret. They decided to return to where they had left the child and take her back. As mentioned in the book, *Nur Jahan: Empress of Mughal India,* they found the child exactly where they had left her, and next to her was a black snake. The child was unharmed.

Perhaps this story will help people make sense of how a child who was nearly abandoned went on to influence the history of Mughal India. Perhaps, this hints at how the child was destined to change the fortunes of her family. It was not long after she was reclaimed that her parents found a merchant willing to help them out.

The merchant's name was Malik Masud, and he also happened to be on his way to Emperor Akbar's court. Some oral accounts suggest that it was Malik Masud who had found the child after the parents left her. Regardless, she was reunited with her parents.

This child was named Mehr-un-nissa, meaning 'sun among women'. With her parents and older siblings, Mehr crossed into Akbar's domain with Malik Masud. This marked the most prominent chapter in the lives of not just the Beg family but also in Akbar's lineage.

After spending some time in Lahore, Mirza Beg headed to Fatehpur Sikri with Malik Masud to meet Akbar. Fatehpur Sikri was Akbar's capital for some time. This was where Malik introduced Mirza Beg to Akbar. Following the footsteps of his father, Mirza Beg joined the royal court. Over time, he went on to become royal treasurer for Kabul.

There came a time when Akbar shifted the capital to Lahore, partly because Fatehpur Sikri did not have enough water to provide for the needs of a bustling capital. This business of shifting capitals is always an idea that mankind has toyed with, especially after they exhaust a city's resources. When Akbar moved, the Beg family moved to Agra—the place where Mehr went on to spend much of her young life.

Many boys in Mughal India were pushed to learn from tutors, but there was no such move for girls from royal bloodlines (regardless of whether they were Hindu or Muslim). However, Mehr grew up writing fine Persian poetry, which indicates that her parents were in favour of ensuring that their daughters were also educated. Jahangir, in his memoirs, described Mirza Beg as a scholar with a 'pretty taste for poetry'. The Begs had a fair share of poets in their family, particularly on Mirza Beg's side. Perhaps another reason why Mehr grew up appreciating poetry is because her father opened up their residence to support poets who later even impressed Jahangir.[2]

There is a debate that has assailed scholars and philosophers for a long time—the question of 'nature versus nurture'. The trajectory of Mirza Beg and Asmat Begum's family only adds fodder to this debate. On the one hand, one of their sons (Asaf Khan) went on to be executed for treason. Another became a loyalist of Shah Jahan. Mirza Beg's daughters grew up to marry nobles too. These women likely had a strong presence—in fact, Manija's (the elder daughter) husband went on to be called 'Qasim Khan Manija', with his wife's name being added to his own.[3]

After a childhood where she developed a fondness for poetry and watched her father's influence grow in the royal court, Mehr's parents found a match for her. In 1594, Mirza Beg's haveli was decked with flowers. Many retellings mention that people were going in and out of Mirza Beg's haveli in their finest of clothes while Mehr

---

[2]Swamy, K.R.N., 'A Mughal Empress' Tribute to Her Father', *The Tribune*, 2 December 2001, https://tinyurl.com/5n9y23kp. Accessed on 25 June 2023.

[3]Beveridge, H., *Maathir-Ul-Umara: Being Biographies of the Muhammadan and Hindu Officers of the Timurid Sovereigns of India from 1500 to about 1780 A.D. (Vol. II)*, The Asiatic Society, 2003.

sat inside, her eyes lined with kohl.

Finding a suitable husband for Mehr must not have been particularly difficult for Mirza Beg as he was a man of high standing.

Besides, tales of Mehr's beauty and talents were aplenty. She was fluent in Arabic and Persian and also excelled in literature and the arts, including music and dance. According to poet and writer Vidya Dhar Mahajan, even though she was known for her volatile temper, the charismatic she largely acted out of common sense and had a certain 'piercing intelligence'.[4] According to writer Abraham Eraly, Mehr was 17 when she was married.

Mehr's groom was Ali Quli Khan Istajlu, who, much like Mehr herself, traced his ancestry back to Iran (from where he had fled to Kandahar before finding a new life in Hindustan). According to historian Abraham Eraly, he was a former table attendant of Shah Ismail of Persia.

Soon after the wedding, the couple left for Burdwan (modern day Bardhaman) in Bengal, where Ali had a new posting as the *jagirdar*. He was now tasked with the area's judicial and police duties, among other things. It is believed that during this time, the young Mehr went through the trauma of suffering several miscarriages. Finally in 1605, Mehr and Ali finally became parents. A

---

[4]Mahajan, Vidya Dhar, *History of Medieval India: Muslim Rule in India–Sultanate Period Mughal Period*, S. Chand Publications, 2018.

daughter was born to them and they named her Ladli Begum.

ᔕ

Ali is described in Abraham Eraly's *Emperors of the Peacock Throne* as a 'strapping young man'. He is also described to be 'a great soldier, but hot-tempered and tactless, with a restless ambition that would not bide its time'.[5] Perhaps it was in the throes of a mix of ambition, temper and tactlessness that Ali went and fought a tiger unarmed. He subdued the beast, winning a new name from Jahangir. After the tiger incident, Ali came to be known as 'Sher Afghan Ali Quli Istajlu' (it roughly translates to the grappler of tigers). He is more popularly known as Sher Afghan Khan. One oral account suggests that he was given the name because he displayed exemplary courage in a battle with a Rajput prince in Mewar.

It is believed that Ali spent long periods of time away from home. During this time, Mehr was left in the company of their daughter and Dilbar Dai (a wet nurse who brought up Mehr). It is also believed that it was here that Mehr honed her expertise with guns. It was also in Bardhaman, in a setting away from her family and everything she had known, that Mehr developed

---

[5]Eraly, Abraham, *Emperors of the Peacock Throne: The Saga of the Great Mughals*, Penguin India, 2007.

administrative skills and an understanding of politics that helped her in the future.

In the Mughal capital, things were changing drastically in the early 1600s. The situation concerned Jahangir. Akbar and Jahangir's relationship soured, and Jahangir began making attempts to take control of his father's throne. This further set off a chain of events that changed the course of Mehr's life.

Helping Akbar and Jahangir negotiate a settlement when they were on the outs was Ruqaiya Sultan Begum, Akbar's first wife and chief consort. A stepmother to Jahangir, she is also believed to have paved the way for his succession.

After Akbar's death, Jahangir ascended his father's throne. Soon after, the relationship between Mehr's husband and the Mughal crown also began to go downhill. Perhaps the very traits that consumed Ali to fight a tiger also resulted in the crown being suspicious of him. These suspicions enveloped him like a blanket. It is likely that the Mughal crown was suspicious that he was sympathetic to the cause of Afghans, and would rebel against the Mughal Empire.

In 1607, Jahangir sent Qutbuddin Khan (the then governor of Bengal) to confirm these rumours. The episode ended with swords covered in blood and death. Ali killed the governor. But there was more that changed that day. The governor's guards avenged his death then and there. About 13 years after she was married to Ali, Mehr was a widow and a single mother.

Shortly after her husband's death, Mehr made her way to Agra. She was accompanied by her daughter Ladli and Dilbar Dai.

∽

Well before fortune favoured the Beg family in Hindustan, Akbar had created a harem with towering walls and spacious rooms for women of the royal household. Thousands of women of all ranks lived there.

Among these women was Ruqaiya Sultan Begum—the same woman who had wielded influence on both Akbar and Jahangir. As she had no biological children of her own, Ruqaiya Begum virtually adopted Jahangir's son Khurram (the man who would later be known as Shah Jahan).

The road from Bengal eventually led Mehr, probably because of her family's influence, to Ruqaiya Begum's doors at the harem. Here she received the protection of many senior women. Some believe that she became a lady-in-waiting for Ruqaiya Begum. Other retellings mention that she was a confidante to senior women in the harem. Either way, she carried out her roles at the harem excellently for four years.

Jahangir had been married several times by then. His youngest son, Shahryar Mirza, was born the year Jahangir took Akbar's throne. It appears that Jahangir's eldest son, Khusrau Mirza, felt he was better suited to sit on the throne than his father. Therefore, relations between the two were complicated.

It was during this time that Mehr first met Jahangir. The most popular retelling of Mehr meeting Jahangir speaks of it taking place in the crowded backdrop of a bustling bazaar. However, the most starry-eyed of the lot is the one written by nineteenth-century Urdu writer Muhammad Husain Azad. He writes in *Darbar-e-Akbari* about an episode when Jahangir was walking back from Meena Bazaar (an imperial bazaar his father had started). This bazaar was a place for elaborate exhibitions, and saw the sale of exquisite things that travelling merchants had collected from across the world. The exhibitions were largely affairs for nobles and royals, and were often frequented by women living in the Mughal harem. At some point or another, women from the harem could be found walking the aisles of the bazaar. Having purchased a pair of particularly exquisite pigeons, Jahangir was walking back home when he spotted a flower that he wanted. Since both his hands were full, he is said to have asked a woman passing by to hold the birds for him while he got the flower.

Having plucked the flower, he turned around to see the woman holding only one bird. On asking where the other went, she replied that it flew away. 'How?', asked the Emperor. 'Like this,' said the woman as she let the second pigeon fly away. This woman was Mehr, of course.[6]

---

[6]Hussain Azad, Mulvi Muhammad, *Darbar-e-Akbari*, Kapoor Art Printing

Only two months later, in 1611, the two were married and Mehr-un-Nissa was renamed Nur Mahal, meaning 'light of the palace'. Five years after this, she was given another name—the name that would stick with her through time—Nur Jahan, meaning 'light of the world'.

It was likely that this was seen as a highly controversial union considering that Jahangir's newest bride was in her mid-30s when the two married. Moreover, she was a widow and a mother.

Such unions make for prime fodder for the imagination. Some stories that have been passed down over generations say that Jahangir had long been enamoured with this young woman's beauty and talents. Some retellings even suggest that he was the one who had her husband killed so that he could have a future with her. This theory does not really hold any water since the two were wed four years after her being on the royal court's premises.

Some oral retellings also say that Nur Jahan was an inspiration to many. Some believe Nur Jahan to be an inspiration for the fictional Anarkali. The only distinction being the background of Anarkali, who was shown to be a courtesan in the brutal story that played out in cinema halls. This story sees Anarkali being buried alive on the orders of the prince's angry father, Akbar.

Works, 1921.

Of course, Anarkali's story is neither present in *Akbarnama* nor in Jahangir's records, because it was originally written by Abdul Halim Sharar. He was a playwright and historian from Lucknow, who clearly mentions in the beginning of his well-loved work that Anarkali's story is a work of fiction.[7]

Putting aside all the stories that have blended so seamlessly, the one thing that we do know is that Nur Jahan was the twentieth wife of Jahangir. She was also the last woman he ever married.

In *Shah Jahan: The Rise and Fall of the Mughal Emperor*, journalist Fergus Nicoll writes about how Nur Jahan 'polarized opinion at court, prompting slavish loyalty from her own supporters and equally venomous disapproval from her critics'.[8] This is true for many rulers, Mughal or otherwise, who had a mind of their own.

That Mirza Beg's association with his rebellious son, Muhammad Sharif, was forgiven and his position solidified again in the Mughal court could also have something to do with Nur Jahan's influence. According to Findly, both her brothers (Asaf Khan and Ibrahim) also continued to be senior officers of the Mughal court, and her extended family had control over Lahore, Kashmir, Odisha, Awadh and Bengal.

---

[7]Gupta, Subhadra Sen, *Mahal: Power and Pageantry in the Mughal Harem*, Hachette India, 2009.

[8]Nicoll, Fergus, *Shah-Jahan: The Rise and Fall of the Mughal Emperor*, Penguin India, 2018.

While many speak of her beauty, Nur Jahan's witty replies to Jahangir paint her as a thinker and someone unafraid to speak her mind. Much like other female writers from the Mughal empire, Nur Jahan also wrote under a pen name. Hers was Makhfi, meaning the 'hidden' or 'veiled one'.[9] Once when Jahangir wondered, 'Why do old men go about with their backs bent?' Nur Jahan promptly replied: 'They are searching in dust for the days of their youth.'[10] Both Jahangir and Nur Jahan loved the beauty of Lahore. The Empress once wrote about this as well: 'We have purchased Lahore with our soul; we have given our life and brought another paradise.'[11]

Such was her love for books that she once spent three gold *mohurs* (coins), a pricey sum, for the manuscript of *Diwan-i-Kamran* (a collection of poems written by Kamran Mirza). The book still lies in the Khuda Baksh Oriental Public Library in Patna.[12]

According to author Ruby Lal in *Empress: The Astonishing Reign of Nur Jahan*, Jahangir was a prolific writer who kept detailed records of gifts he received (peaches as 'big as an owl's head') and of the time he met Nur

---

[9]Lal, Ruby, *Empress: The Astonishing Reign of Nur Jahan*, Penguin India Viking, 2018.

[10]Ibid.

[11]Findly, Ellison Banks, *Nur Jahan: The Empress of India*, Oxford University Press, 1993.

[12]Baqa, Shabistan, *A Critical Edition of Diwan-e-Mirza Kamran (Persian Text) with Introduction and Notes*, Aligarh Muslim University, 2005.

Jahan's family. However, there is no mention of the woman herself. According to Ruby Lal, when he finally does mention her in 1614, it's a 'remarkable record' that paints a flattering portrait of Nur Jahan as a caregiver, diplomat, hunter, athlete and more.[13]

Her strength and presence in the Mughal household, and by extension in the Mughal kingdom, continued to grow. Known for her aesthetic sense, she dictated fashion trends and popularized brocades and laces of various kinds. She was also noticed for her generosity as she helped the less fortunate. She gave gifts of horses, jewels and elephants to those around her. Nur Jahan also took it upon herself to make sure that orphaned girls lacking financial support system had a proper wedding. She got at least 500 ceremonies conducted. She also designed the Nur Mahali—an inexpensive wedding dress set one could get for both the bride and the groom.[14]

Nur Jahan's interest in the arts meant that artisans were called to court from far and wide. She herself was good with needlework. The art of *chikankari* thrived during her time, as did *badla* (a silver-threaded brocade) and *kinari* (a silver-threaded lace).

According to the Italian traveller Niccolao Manucci, the credit for *attar* or *itr* (perfume) also goes to Nur

---

[13]Lal, Ruby, *Empress: The Astonishing Reign of Nur Jahan*, Penguin India Viking, 2018.

[14]Findly, Ellison Banks, *Nur Jahan: The Empress of India*, Oxford University Press, 1993.

Jahan.[15] But according to Jahangir's documents, that honour actually goes to Nur Jahan's mother. These documents mention an instance when Asmat Begum was making rose water when she noticed a thick, oily layer on the surface of the pots where hot rose water had been kept overnight. This chance observation eventually led to distilling for itr. The strength of this was such that if a single drop touched the palm of one's hand, its 'scents a whole assembly and it appears as if many rose buds had bloomed together at once. There is no other scent of equal excellence. It restores hearts that have broken and brings back withered souls. In reward for its invention, I presented the maker a string of pearls.'[16]

Food historians such as Salma Hussain have credited Nur Jahan with the introduction of delightful *sharbats* in the Mughal court. Yes, practitioners of herbal medicines had been concocting drinks from flowers, fruits and herbs but these were largely for medicinal purposes. It was Nur Jahan who wanted to 'taste' the roses she was so fond of. The empress is also credited with fusing mango nectar with roses to create wines.[17]

Some oral stories even credit the invention of the biryani to her but there's no official record of this. Meat

---

[15]Manucci, Niccolò, *Storia do Mogor: or, Mogul India, 1653–1708*, William Irvine (trans.), Editions Indian, 1965.

[16]Thackston, Wheeler McIntosh, *The Jahangirnama: Memoirs of Jahangir, Emperor of India*, Facsimile Publisher, 2016.

[17]Hussain, Salma, *50 Great Recipes: Sharbats*, Roli & Janssen, 2005.

with rice and spices was already a common preparation in Mughal India and there exists a word in Persian, *birinj biryani*—which translates to fried rice.[18]

That said, Nur Jahan does get credit for adding to the grandiosity of tastes as well as presentation of food. One time, for instance, she had curd set in seven moulds with rainbow-coloured fruit juices. She would also garnish dishes with floral patterns made with powdered and glazed rice paste.

∽

It has been easy, far too easy, to dismiss Nur Jahan as nothing but the romantic interest of a Mughal emperor and as a woman who lived in the harem. But she was his co-sovereign.

One indication of her political power was the introduction of coins bearing her name. In fact, no other female Mughal royal has had coins issued in their name. These were in gold as well as silver. Some of them, like Jahangir's coins, even had the signs of the zodiac on them. The gold ones read, 'By order of King Jahangir, gold has a hundred splendours added to it by receiving the impression of Nur Jahan, the Queen Begam.'[19]

---

[18]'From Iran to India: The Journey and Evolution of Biriyani', *BBC*, 16 July 2016, https://tinyurl.com/yckezfr3. Accessed on 23 June 2023.
[19]Lal, Ruby, *Empress: The Astonishing Reign of Nur Jahan*, Penguin India Viking, 2018.

Distributed across Mughal cities, ranging from Agra and Ahmadabad (Ahmedabad) to Lahore, these coins were quite a collectors' item.

Jahangir experimented with zodiac coins, coins featuring couplets and coins with Nur Jahan's face; his father, Akbar, had a similar interest in coins. The coins minted under Akbar even had embossing ducks and hawks. Jahangir's successor did not care for these coins. He had most of them melted down, so the ones that are still in existence are a rare collectors' item.

Like those who came before and after her, Nur Jahan's influence as a co-sovereign was belittled by a fair share of people. An Italian musicologist, Pietro Della Valle, after being disappointed with his own love life, travelled across modern day Turkey, Egypt, Persia and India between 1614 and 1628. He makes a rather nasty mention of Nur Jahan in his writings. It goes as follows:

> And as such she commands and governs as this day in the king's Haram (harem) with supreme authority; having cunningly removed out of the Haram, either by marriage, or other handsome wages, all other women who might have give(n) her jealousies [sic]; and also in the Court made alterations by deposing, and displacing almost all the old Captains and officers...[20]

---

[20]Grey, Edward (ed.), *The Travels of Pietro Della Valle in India: From the Old English Translation of 1664*, B. Franklin, 1892.

On seeing a woman wielding power, Della Valle wrote that Nur Jahan had 'cunningly' ensured the removal of women she was insecure about, besides displacing Jahangir's loyalists at the Mughal court. To those who play down Nur Jahan's actual influence and power, the role she played when the Emperor was in physical danger—imprisoned by a foe who was once a friend—comes as proof of the true extent of her involvement in the kingdom.

As Jahangir had done once before with his father, Akbar, his own sons threatened Jahangir's throne. There were many contenders for the throne and these rifts were obvious enough for all to see. For instance, the rifts were visible when Mahabat Khan (a Mughal statesperson and general, previously a Jahangir loyalist who had been well honoured in the past) led a coup to unseat Jahangir.

Three years before this, Mahabat Khan had led an unsuccessful rebellion against the person threatening Jahangir's emperorship the most, Prince Khurram. Mahabat Khan lost that battle but his power in the Mughal court continued to grow.

According to Findly, Mahabat Khan was wary of Nur Jahan's influence. This was a well-known sentiment and he had supposedly even shared this with Jahangir. The dislike was mutual. Nur Jahan disapproved of the growing warmth between Mahabat Khan and Parviz Mirza (another son of Jahangir and another contender for the throne).[21]

Distance is one way of putting relationships and alliances to the test. To break the alliance between Mahabat Khan and Parviz Mirza, the former was sent to Bengal as a governor—a posting that neither of them took well. Mahabat Khan had been asked to give an account of how he used money given to him when he had gone up in battle against Shah Jahan before. Mahabat Khan was likely furious about this, and it is possible that he saw this as them questioning his loyalty. Then he marched from Ranthambore to see Jahangir.

Mahabat Khan was accompanied by 4,000–5,000 Rajput soldiers. He sent his son-in-law ahead, with a letter expressing how he was ready 'to hand over his wives and children as a pledge, but couldn't permit himself to be dragged into the royal presence like a guilty criminal'.[22] One wonders if Mahabat Khan's ego or honour was far greater than the safety and well-being of his family or whether he had absolute faith that Jahangir wouldn't harm them. Findly records in her book that Mahabat Khan wasn't happy about Jahangir trusting Nur Jahan with court affairs as much as he did.

According to the *Jahangirnama*, once Jahangir and Nur Jahan were travelling from Lahore to Kabul and had stopped to camp by the waters of the Jhelum. Before

---

[21]Findly, Ellison Banks, *Nur Jahan: The Empress of India*, Oxford University Press, 1993.
[22]Ibid.

dawn, Mahabat Khan went into the Emperor's tent and likely threatened him to put on an act. If anyone asked, Jahangir was supposed to tell them they were going out to hunt. The ruse worked and before anyone could apprehend what was happening, Jahangir was already in confinement and guarded by Mahabat Khan's men. Mahabat Khan then sent his men back to capture Nur Jahan too. Disguised as a commoner, Nur Jahan had already crossed a bridge across the river and met up with her brother, Asaf Khan. She then gathered all the nobles together and gave them an earful for the lax security conditions, which had enabled the Emperor's abduction. A plan was formed to secure Jahangir's freedom.

When the day of battle to get Jahangir out of Mahabat Khan's grasp finally arrived, Nur Jahan was in the middle of it all—riding atop an elephant. She had by her side her daughter, Ladli, as well as her granddaughter.

According to Findly, Nur Jahan was there to free her husband, but she also looked out for others on the battlefield. When a woman fighting alongside her was wounded after an arrow pierced her arm, it was Nur Jahan who pulled it out. In blood-stained clothes, she continued to fight for several hours till she and the other leaders realized that the war was going nowhere. They were only losing more and more men, and were no closer to reaching the Emperor's place of captivity. The fact that Asaf Khan had disappeared from the battlefield, possibly taking along with him a few 100 soldiers, was another big blow to Nur Jahan's rescue mission.

Instead of retreating, Nur Jahan, along with Prince Shahryar and a few others, surrendered themselves to Mahabat Khan. He declared himself the Emperor in Kabul, and Jahangir and Nur Jahan didn't put up a fight at that point.

Mahabat Khan then began to believe that he had complete control of things. He decreased the presence of guards who kept a watch on Jahangir and Nur Jahan—an opportunity that Nur Jahan deftly made use of. She recruited men in secret and aligned herself with those who opposed Mahabat Khan. This secret mission paid off, and Mahabat Khan lost the empire he had conspired for—Jahangir wore the imperial crown once again. While it is likely that one of the other people loyal to Jahangir could have helped him re-take his throne, Nur Jahan's involvement is significant in the events that took place.

Mahabat Khan eventually found an unlikely ally—Shah Jahan—the very man whom he had fought against some time ago. Shah Jahan had, by then, expressed clear intentions of taking over his father's throne. He found that though many were loyal to his father, he could still gather support from some of the younger nobles.

The seat of power has always been a fickle friend in a world of shifting alliances—something that even the present-day political landscape has in common with Nur Jahan's time. Even as Shah Jahan's alliance with Mahabat Khan strengthened, Jahangir was growing ill in the heat of

Lahore. In 1627, those at Jahangir's court—in the hopes that a cooler climate would do him some good—decided to move to Kashmir.

Jahangir could no longer ride a horse and had to be carried in a palki. He refused to eat food and even rejected opium, his chief vice.

Such were the wheels of fate that sickness came knocking on another door as well. Prince Shahryar, the heir apparent till then, fell ill. He lost all his hair, including his eyelashes and eyebrows. So the royal party decided to return to Lahore, hoping to find a cure to manage his condition. They split up, with Prince Shahryar going back first. While Jahangir and Nur Jahan were making their own return journey, tragedy struck.

Shortly after they had crossed Rajouri, the news broke that Jahangir was no more. Nur became a widow for the second time.

There was more grief in store for Nur Jahan. Asaf Khan, once her trusted aide, now stood on the opposing side. He had abandoned Nur and her soldiers on the battlefield before and now he openly sided with the enemy.

It's likely that Asaf Khan didn't want Nur Jahan to place the ailing Shahryar on the throne, and that's why he assigned guards to keep a close watch on his sister. While Jahangir's body was being taken for funeral rites, Nur Jahan was allowed (under strict guard) to follow the procession.

Meanwhile in Lahore, with the blessings of Nur Jahan,

Shahryar announced himself as his father's successor. But since he was unwell, not many had faith in him. Days after his announcement, Asaf Khan's men had him in chains. He was blinded and imprisoned.

In 1628, Shah Jahan ascended to the throne at Lahore. According to Findly, Asaf Khan had Shahryar and the sons of two of his own brothers executed, to ensure that there was no other contender to the throne. That's what it took for Shah Jahan to become emperor.

Asaf Khan allowed Nur Jahan to spend the remainder of her life in seclusion in Lahore. It's possible he felt that she wouldn't be able to cause him trouble if she was sent away. This life in exile lasted for 18 years and we know very little of what went on then. Historians believe that she accepted this life, continuing to give to charity. She was often seen, with her attendants in tow, at her husband Jahangir's tomb.

∽

At a time when a woman's worth was cemented by the heirs she birthed, Nur Jahan gave Jahangir no children. And yet, the influence she had on him remains a matter of record with Jahangir noting her personal contributions to his life. She had, to a certain degree, been able to reduce his wine intake and ensure he ate healthier. Some would like to paint her as a power-hungry woman but the administrative abilities of this elegant, thoughtful and quick-witted woman made up for Jahangir's shortcomings.

Her well-rounded attributes extended to everyday affairs of the court too. Nur Jahan was more than just a fashionable and hospitable wife, she also proved to be an able commander of forces and a strategic planner when it came to rescuing Jahangir. When she was not involved in charitable deeds—like finding partners for orphaned young women—she helped artisans secure their livelihood by popularizing embroidery techniques. She also made time to get involved with several marvels of architecture that have stood the test of time.[23]

Among the many architectural marvels made under the supervision of Nur Jahan is the tomb of Itimad-ud-Daula. Sometimes called the Bachcha Mahal (or even the 'Baby Taj'), this holds the remains of Nur Jahan's parents. Often considered to be an inspiration for Taj Mahal with its finely carved marble jaalis (lattice screens), it is also located in Agra. As opposed to the regular red sandstone, this is believed to be one of the first Mughal tombs built near the Yamuna in polished white marble.

Then there's the Achabal Gardens in Anantnag in the Kashmir Valley, now a small public park, which owes its creation to her. She also built several *serai*s or rest houses for travellers, including the Serai Nurmahal or

---

[23]Safvi, Rana, 'Was Nur Jahan a Scheming Temptress or Just an Independent Woman Who Historians Couldn't Fathom?', *Scroll.in*, 8 March 2016, https://tinyurl.com/3zbm3ezp. Accessed on 25 June 2023.

the Mughal Serai near the city of Jalandhar.

After his death, Jahangir was brought to Dilkusha Gardens (also known as Shahdara Bagh), one of Nur Jahan's favourite places in Lahore. His remains were buried there, along the banks of the Ravi.

Despite all her accomplishments, many have painted Nur Jahan in an unflattering light. Satish Chandra, an expert in medieval Indian history, believes that much of this is because of sheer 'prejudice' against the Empress. According to him: 'The charge of meddling in imperial affairs leading to disaffection and rebellion, reflected the deep-seated anti-feminist bias of many contemporary historians which has often been repeated uncritically by a number of modern historians.'[24]

As if to wipe away all memory of Nur Jahan, Shah Jahan had all coins that were stamped in her name withdrawn from circulation. Her life in exile ended when she passed away on 18 December 1645. She was 72. She lies buried in a red sandstone mausoleum in Shahdara Bagh that she designed herself.

Flower mosaics in semi-precious stones adorned this mausoleum on the banks of the Ravi—the same banks on which Nur Jahan and Jahangir once walked.[25] The place was surrounded by a garden of tulips, roses and jasmine.

---

[24]Chandra, Satish, *Medieval India: From Sultanat to the Mughals- Mughal Empire (1526–1748)*, Har Anand Publications, 2007.

[25]Naravane, Susheila, *Acute Akbar Versus the Spirited Nur Jahan: The Soul's Journey Through Time and the Who's Who*, Troubador Publishing, 2018.

Her epitaph, for which she chose the words herself, reads as follows: 'On the grave of this poor stranger, let there be neither lamp nor rose. This way, neither will the wings of moth burn, nor will nightingales sing.'[26]

It is believed that the adornments and marble from Nur Jahan's tomb were removed during the expansion of the Sikh Empire. The plundering continued well into the reign of Maharaja Ranjit Singh (grandfather of Princess Sophia Duleep Singh). Years later, when a railway line was built under British rule, it separated Nur Jahan's tomb from the tombs of her family members.[27]

Alexander Dow, a writer and an officer of the EIC, wrote the following lines about Nur Jahan: 'The power (of women), it is true, is sometimes exerted in the harem; but, like the virtues of a magnet, it is silent and unperceived. Nur Jahan stood forth in public; she broke through all restraints and custom, and acquired power by her own address, more than by the weakness of Jahangir.'[28]

As historian Tahera Aftab mentions in the English translation of *Life of Nur Jahan Begam* (written by Nawab Imad Nawaz Jang in 1892): 'Those who oppose women's education or who want to make efforts to restrict women's

---

[26]Lal, Ruby, *Empress: The Astonishing Reign of Nur Jahan*, Penguin India Viking, 2018.

[27]Sheikh, Majid, 'Harking Back: Once the "Pride of Lahore"—Now a Classy Carcass', *Dawn*, 29 March 2020, https://tinyurl.com/mr34jbu6. Accessed on 23 June 2023.

[28]Dow, Alexander, *The History of Hindostan, Volume III*, T. Becket and P.A. De Hondt, London, 1772.

proficiency to a few religious texts, or those groups who think that Nature, compared to men, has endowed women with incomplete faculties, all of them must reform their misunderstanding by the life story of Nur Jahan.'[29]

Travel across the areas that comprised Hindustan, from Lahore to Bengal, and Nur Jahan's stories—of how she killed a tiger and saved a village; how Nur Jahan and Jahangir were star-crossed lovers; and how she rode an elephant into battle to rescue an imprisoned Emperor—continue to be told as tales of yore. If you ever find yourself at Taj Mahal, dear reader, marvelling at Shah Jahan's declaration of love—think also of those who lost their lives for the fickle throne. And if you ever find yourself at Nur Jahan's grave in Lahore, dear reader, ask yourself what she must have been thinking when she said no one should burn candles or strew roses on her grave.

[29]Aftab, Tahera, *Inscribing South Asian Muslim Women: An Annotated Bibliography & Research Guide*, Brill, 2008.

Didda

The Shaper of a Dynasty

KASHMIR, 958

The flames continued to dance as scores of people watched. Some of them wept. Others stood and observed the scene unfold from a distance. The heat from the fire had already begun to charge the air, warming those who stood close to the fire.

The King's body was already consumed by flames. His courtiers stood closest to the fire, but even those who didn't work at the court had come out to pay their respects on this solemn occasion. This was a day they would talk about for years to come as the King's last rites were only part of the ceremonies for the day. The funeral ceremonies were far from being over as the Queens were yet to walk into the fire.

If a Queen had died, the King could have just

taken another Queen in her stead at a time he deemed appropriate. But there could be no life for a married woman after her husband died. As the customs dictated, she was expected to walk into her husband's funeral pyre.

One of the Queens making this fateful walk was Chief Minister Phalguna's daughter, Chandralekha. It did not take her very long to walk into the fire, though it did take time for the flames to fully consume her life force. These proceedings marked a significant event in Kashmir's history—the death of King Kshemagupta.

Then came the moment that would mark the ending of the funeral. It was time for the King's favourite wife, Didda (a Princess of the Loharin kingdom), to follow the other Queens.

Much before the funeral processions had started, Phalguna had tried to console Didda. He had told her that the throne of Kashmir would be safe under his guardianship, and that he would personally watch over Abhimanyu—the heir to the throne of Kashmir and Didda and Kshemagupta's son.

Abhimanyu was a young lad, and he had not been crowned yet. Phalguna assured her that she could just be the grieving wife and embrace death.

Naravahana, one of the King's aides, tried to

convince Didda to do the opposite of what Phalguna was suggesting. According to the book *Rajatarangini* by Kalhan, Naravahana wanted to stop Didda from performing sati. But it seemed like Didda would perish along with the King's mortal remains before the day was done.

This was the same Didda who was equally famous for her beauty as she was for her walk—she had a limp. In fact, a historian of those times went as far as to refer to Didda as *charanhina* (footless).

The grieving Queen took a good look around. High-born nobles from the court surrounded them, as did their families. As the funeral pyre waited to claim her, Didda thought not just about herself, but also her son. She thought of how little he was and of the world they lived in.

Didda then turned towards the Chief Minister and said, 'You could not protect your own daughter Chandralekha, how can you take care of my son?'[1] Didda decided that the funeral pyre would not consume her. Then, to everyone's shock, Didda announced that she was returning to the court as it was her duty to claim her late husband's throne. She did so in her son's name.

---

[1]Garodia Gupta, Archana, *The Women Who Ruled India: Leaders. Warriors. Icons.*, Hachette India, 2019.

DIDDA'S STORY

High up on a hill, somewhere most likely in the Pir Panjal range of the mighty Himalayas, stood a fortress called Loharkot. This was home to the kings and queens of the Lohara dynasty.

Beautiful little villages, straight out of a dream, marked the kingdom of Lohara, which included modern-day Poonch in Kashmir too. Since the place was on the trade route between Punjab and Kashmir, it was routinely swept up in the hustle bustle brought in by traders and travellers.

Even as time passes swiftly during routine affairs, every once in a while there are moments when life comes to a pause. This leads to a subtle change in the rhythm of things. For instance, the two ends of the throbbing cycle of life—birth and death—makes us put everything on hold.

It was the former of the two ends—a birth—that had made the court of Simharaja (the King of Lohara) pause in the midst of their courtly affairs. Even as the attendants and courtiers prayed for the health of their queen and the birth of a healthy child, those in the know had a feeling that Simharaja was hoping for a princess. He already had a number of sons who could secure his family's control over the throne, but there was not a single girl in the family. It is quite possible that he was open to a change.

In another palace, another king, Bhimadeva, was waiting to hear of any news coming from Simharaja's court. Bhimadeva belonged to the Hindu Shahi dynasty. He was part of one of the last Hindu dynasties to rule over Gandhara and Kabul Valley in medieval India.

In the present day, the area commanded by the Shahi dynasty falls within the confines of modern-day Pakistan and Afghanistan. The reason Bhimadeva was so concerned about the affairs of another kingdom was because Simharaja's queen was Bhimadeva's daughter. Any child born to Simharaja would also be a child of the Hindu Shahi kingdom.

It is safe to assume that there was a certain degree of nervousness among the people waiting to hear from the Queen's quarters. It's possible that the nervousness was quelled when the cries of a newborn babe reached their ears. The kingdom had a new royal and after many moons of prayers and much anticipation—the kingdom had its princess. But if only this were a regular story.

The Princess had come into a world of great expectations but it started on a bad foot, literally. Her gait would never be straight and she would always have a limp. This limp could not be fixed even by the best of the king's healers. As the word spread (gossip grapevines have always existed), the celebrations in Lohara were likely to be muted. One imagines that the celebrations faded away to nothingness, especially compared to the grand episodes that unfolded when her elder brothers were born.

Many believe that Simharaja could not quite accept his daughter's fate. One retelling of the story suggests that he weighed all his choices and wondered if his child should even live with a physical disability. But doubts aside, her life was spared. Call it luck or the making of destiny, but she lived to be strong and healthy. This princess was named 'Didda'.

Being a princess meant many pleasures were guaranteed to her, but Didda's life was different from that of a regular member of the royal court. Though she roamed about freely and had everything riches could offer, one imagines she longed for the affection of her parents. The unusual forming of her foot kept her from the kind of attention a princess would receive. She existed, but it seemed best if her existence was limited to the shadows alone.

∽

They say a person's childhood shapes their future. It creates the hazy outlines of who one might become. The chapters from Didda's childhood are a testament to this.

When there were sporting events in the kingdom, for instance, one would expect the princess to be mere a spectator in the games. But Didda was not one to watch the world go by without taking a slice of what she was owed. Despite knowing that she was different from others, it is likely that Didda refused to feel sorry for herself.

She grew up to be adept in archery, sword fighting as well as horseback riding.

When the sporting events in the kingdom began, Didda participated in them wholeheartedly. When she was not charging towards the finish line on horseback, she was competing among the best archers in the kingdom. Even a foot race could not dissuade Didda. If she was a sight on horseback, she made for a remarkable (if not shocking) sight as she joined these foot races. And because she herself could not run a foot race efficiently, Didda would piggyback on a tall, sturdy woman.

This woman, reportedly of African origin, was called Valaga. She was at once Didda's unofficial guardian and her support system. She was her closest confidante. Even when her parents were unsure of how to deal with Didda's physical challenges, it was Valaga who often guided her thoughts and actions. She taught Didda to be fearless. Valaga taught the child that her bad foot was no reason to hold herself back, and Didda learnt that lesson well.

Didda even watched her father work from the sidelines, quietly learning how he conducted and resolved the affairs of the court. It was in this way that she learned the nuances of diplomacy and how to run a kingdom. If her bad foot meant she could not lead the conventional life of a princess, it also meant that she could focus her energy to develop skills that would serve her well in an uncertain and ever-shifting future.

Didda was unmarried well into her 20s—a great

sacrilege in those times. But little did anyone know that Didda's life was about to change dramatically. In the words of historian Prem Nath Bazaz: 'Though she was lame, the beauty of her face and the grace of her form were enchanting.'[2]

ᔕ

In a kingdom not very far away, another King was lost in deep thought. This was the King of Kashmir, Kshemagupta. Intellectuals in his capital city suspected that Kshemagupta did not really care about the kingdom or its people. He seemed to care more for intoxicants, and spent a good number of days hunting. Perhaps, he even knew this himself. The one thing he did care about was the throne. To keep that, he needed a male heir. A boy who would ensure that his hold on the throne stayed firm.

He had already married Chandralekha, the daughter of his chief minister. But since there were no sons from his union, Kshemagupta was open to another match.

The day Didda crossed paths with Kshemagupta was the day when not just their fortunes, but even the course of the history of Kashmir changed. Kshemagupta, who had taken over the kingdom from his father in 950 CE,

[2]Bazaz, Prem Nath, *Daughters of the Vitasta: A History of Kashmiri Women from Early Times to the Present Day*, Pamposh Publications, 1959.

was enchanted by Didda's beauty.

The King of Kashmir had a decision to make. Could he really take a woman who had one bad foot and make her his queen? Marrying Didda meant that he would also have the backing of the Shahi dynasty since she was Bhimadeva's granddaughter. Politically, it was a good move.

Having multiple wives has long been associated with the Mughal kings alone, but even otherwise, it was a common practice in India.

It's likely that Simharaja was more than happy to accept any proposal for Didda's hand in marriage. Many princes had previously declined to marry Didda. Her advancing age (according to that period) had not helped things either. And here was Kshemagupta wanting to marry her. She was 26 at the time of the wedding.[3]

If her life before the wedding was eventful, marked with unforgettable races as she rode on Valaga's back, the years that followed were even more dramatic. Through Didda's union with Kshemagupta, two territories were united and Didda became the Queen of Kashmir. Srinagar was her new home.

A woman who piggybacked for foot races and who was shunned by her potential suitors was now in power in one of the most beautiful places of the world. But beauty has never been any guarantee against pain, blood or

[3]Garodia Gupta, Archana, 'Didda, Controversial Queen of Kashmir', *Swarajya*, 26 April 2015, https://tinyurl.com/2p8wyk6n. Accessed on 23 June 2023.

betrayal. Didda's story went on to become proof of that.

The history of Kshemagupta and Didda—the Kashmiri Hindu rulers of the northernmost fringes of Hindustan—comes to us from the book *Kalhana's Rajatarangini: A Chronicle of the Kings of Kashmir.* This work of history was written by Kalhana in the twelfth century. The version of the book used here is by M.A. Stein, a Hungarian-born British archaeologist and a scholar of Kalhana's work, who has translated it into English. Kalhana's work in Sanskrit is often considered to be among the oldest records that chronicle India's history.

Kalhana documented Kashmir's history—from its association with the Mahabharata, right down to the rule of Jayasimha in 1159. This monumental work not just documents the histories of Kashmir's rulers but also the rise of Buddhism in Kashmir.

It is from Kalhana's writing that we know how madly the King had fallen in love with Didda. The two were finally married in 950 CE. As she entered the kingdom that she would eventually wholeheartedly embrace, Didda was given a grand welcome. Standing among all the people were three people significant to Didda's story. One of them was Naravahana, the other Phalguna. The third was Chandralekha.

As Didda entered the palace, hoping her new life would be better than the one she left behind, Chandralekha watched her carefully. She may have been thinking that this new Queen could very well overshadow her influence.

Yes, her father was the King's chief minister—but she worried that Didda would shift the balance of power in the court. And she did!

Kshemagupta was so in love with Didda that he had coins made with the inscription 'Di(dda) Kshemagupta Deva'—a combination of both their names. His people even referred to him as 'Diddakshema', though it is largely suspected this was not done out of respect, but instead as a commentary on how infatuated Kshemagupta was with Didda.[4] This kind of talk was bound to create enemies for Didda. It was unacceptable for a woman to have as much influence over a King as Didda did.

Despite how much Kshemagupta adored his new bride, his pronounced vices—particularly drinking and gambling—meant that he was not very popular with his people. His aide, Naravahana, would often try to nudge him in the right direction but a King ultimately does what he wants to do. As mentioned previously, Naravahana was fond of the new Queen and sided with her.

Then, it finally happened. As Kshemagupta had wanted and wished for so long, Didda gave him a male heir. The birth of a boy meant that his family's claim over the throne of Kashmir was secure. If Didda's birth was awaited, her son's birth was even more so. This son, as we already know, was Abhimanyu.

---

[4]Kalla, Krishnan Lal, *Eminent Personalities of Kashmir,* Discovery Publishing House, 1997.

Life swiftly moved on. In stark contrast to his father's notoriously built-up image, it seemed as if Abhimanyu had a bent towards the Shastras and the holy books even as a young boy.

About eight years after he married Didda, King Kshemagupta contracted an infection. Called '*luta*', this disease covered his body in angry eruptions, rashes and boils that seemed to have a good hold on him. But the fever that followed these eruptions was worse. It just refused to leave. He is said to have caught the disease when he had gone to hunt jackals. Ultimately, he himself became nature's prey. He was then taken to Varahamula (modern-day Baramulla), where he died.[5]

Didda's first order of duty following the King's passing was to immediately send their son Abhimanyu away into hiding. She feared that their enemies would seize this opportunity to make a play for the throne.

This fear had materialized numerous times in royal histories before. Many years ago, almost half a century before, in fact, another queen of Kashmir was in a similar situation. This queen, Sugandhadevi, had accompanied her husband (Shankaravarman) to the battlefield. She saw him getting killed there. When she realized that they were surrounded by feudal lords, veering for a chance to overthrow her family, Sugandhadevi hid the news of

---

[5]Bazaz, Prem Nath, *Daughters of the Vitasta: A History of Kashmiri Women from Early Times to the Present Day*, Pamposh Publications, 1959.

her husband's death. She managed to make them think he was alive and well by tying strings to his body. When the lords went past, offering salutations to the dead king, he was seen acknowledging their greetings. This was all because Sugandhadevi managed to move his limbs, like one could do with a puppet. As Archana Garodia Gupta mentions in her book, Sugandhadevi managed to rule Kashmir for 20 years and was finally overthrown and executed by her own courtiers.

Similarly for Didda, the very first threat came not from other kingdoms but from her own husband's court. As talked about earlier, they kept pushing her to walk into the pyre lit for her husband and she refused on her son's account. She had to live, she said, to protect the future King of Kashmir.

She had many reasons to be suspicious of the people at the court. People were quick to descend on Kshemagupta's wives soon after his death, urging them towards the funeral pyre. Those with political leanings knew that this was the right time to elbow their way to Kashmir's throne. But for this, they first had to get Kshemagupta's queens out of the way. Then, it would be easy to manipulate the young prince. But Didda stumped their plans when she refused to perform sati.

While Kshemagupta's rule was almost insignificant, it was Didda's rule that left an indelible mark on the history of Kashmir. Stories about Kshemagupta focus on how he used to drink heavily. Didda left behind a completely contrasting legacy. But all of that came later.

Before anything else, she had to ensure that the kingdom was safe for her son. She also had to ensure all those who wanted to take advantage of her husband's death were kept at bay.

Knowing friend from foe can be tricky for anyone. But Phalguna and Didda's had never seen eye to eye. Prem Nath Bazaz writes that Phalguna felt Didda bore malice towards him. Considering Didda had already seen how Phalguna had let his own daughter die and was okay with Didda doing so as well, it wouldn't have been hard for other courtiers to add fuel to this tension. There was talk of him having an army, which could challenge the Queen, after all.

After some time, the Queen's messengers informed her that Phalguna had laid down his arms in a temple dedicated to Lord Vishnu. This was a kind of truce for both sides. As mentioned in *Eminent Personalities of Kashmir*, Didda appears to have been a follower of Vishnu. Didda did not call him back and Phalguna did not come back either. There was just too much mistrust between the two for them to face each other.

Back at the court, Didda became the de facto ruler with her son as the King. With Phalguna gone, Naravahana effectively became her chief minister. But she was still surrounded by trouble and deceit from close quarters. As mentioned by Kalhana, one of the greatest threats that Didda ever faced was an uprising led by Mahiman and Patala—two young men who were the sons of the Kshemagupta's sisters.

Mahiman and Patala had grown up in the court and were never treated as anything less than royalty. But as long as Didda and Abhimanyu were around, they could not lay claim to the throne. This is why they forged alliances behind Didda's back, hoping to lead a rebellion against her when the opportunity presented itself. These things are always a matter of timing. Things are never always good or bad for anyone. The two brothers just had to wait for when Didda was weak.

When that time finally came, the brothers realized they had underestimated Didda. All the years of watching her father from the sidelines had turned Didda into a shrewd statesperson. She knew well enough that there were many ways of getting something done. Instead of quenching the rebellion by force, Didda chose to motivate the chief supporters of those rebelling against her financially. Instead of using an army, Didda used the power of gold to get all the people Mahiman and Patala were striking deals with to join her side.

As mentioned in Prem Nath Bazaz's book, 'The lame Queen whom no one had thought capable of stepping over a cow's footprint got over the host of her enemies just as Hanuman got over the ocean.'[6] Everyone had underestimated and written off Didda. But as the Queen

---

[6]Ibid.

of Kashmir, she proved herself over and over.

It was during her reign that the Shaivite philosopher Abhinavagupta (950–1016) wrote many works of significance. These include the *Tantraloka* (Light on Tantra) and *Paramarthasara* (Essence of the Exact Reality).

In his book *Didda: The Warrior Queen of Kashmir*, writer Ashish Kaul sums up how this great saint and yogi Abhinavagupta was won over by Didda's knowledge of the Shastras. This yogi went on to become her adviser in dire times. One such time was when she had to choose between visiting her ailing grandfather, the Shahi King Bhimadeva, and her own son Abhimanyu's coronation.[7]

More rebellions were just around the corner. One night, her palace was besieged by another faction of rebels, and she was trapped. It could have meant death for her if Naravahana and others had not reached the mahal in time and rescued her.

Didda had all the rebels captured and executed as punishment for the attack. Perhaps historians would have been kinder to this act of politics if she were a man. Didda's actions are constantly viewed as a 'woman's actions'. Lest anyone accuse her of being soft, she even had the families of the rebels executed. But she spared some people too, like a man called Yashodhara. He was a reputed warrior, and Didda designated him as

---

[7]Kaul, Ashish, *Didda: The Warrior Queen of Kashmir*, Rupa Publications, 2019.

the commander-in-chief. She then sent him off to face another enemy—the King of a neighbouring kingdom, called Thakkana. Yashodhara was victorious in this battle and chose to let Thakkana live.

He was expecting a hero's welcome when he rode back to the Queen, but things move swifter than the wind in politics. She had spared Yashodhara and even honoured him for fighting on her behalf but was now unsure of where he stood. While he was away from court some courtiers had poisoned Didda's ears against him, according to Kalhana. And with every step Yashodhara and his men took towards the court at Srinagar, Didda's worries grew. She wondered if Yashodhara would try to challenge her, like his family had done once before, especially now that he was emboldened by his win over Thakkana.

Didda finally sent out soldiers to capture him but this attempt failed. An angry Yashodhara then raked up support against her. He got other nobles to join him. This was one of the worst revolts that Didda ever saw but she managed to crush it.

The next target in line was Naravahana. His exalted position had begun to make others wary. Rumours of how Naravahana was not loyal to the throne made their way to Didda too, just as they were meant to.

Naravahana was not unaware of these rumours either. He had started to feel that Didda was giving him the cold shoulder, so he sent out an invite asking her to join him for a meal at his residence. Maybe he felt that a face-to-face talk could help iron things out. But Didda declined his invitation. Naravahana was left heartbroken. After all his years of service to the royal family, he was out of Didda's good books. Thoroughly dispirited, it was not long after this incident that the minister took his own life. For all her faults, Didda was ready to make amends and put her trust in Phalguna after Naravahana's death. There were new threats to the kingdom and Phalguna rejoined her ranks immediately to face these threats.

Death surrounded Didda; it touched everyone she loved but refused to take her. After taking her husband and loyal minister, death sunk its claws into her son Abhimanyu. The young king, who had by now grown up to have three children, fell ill and passed away in 972. His untimely death is likely to have caused immense grief to Didda. She put her grandson, Nandigupta, on the throne as she dealt with the tragedy. There is no right way to react to death. Some are unable to hide their grief; for others, it might be hidden—out of sight but ever present. According to Kalla, Didda's way of dealing with Abhimanyu's death was to spend her days having buildings constructed, particularly temples, in her son's memory. It was a flurry of construction powered by a mother's pain, as if the stones of the temples could somehow channel a dead son's spirit.

She built *matha*s (monasteries) and towns, the most notable of which are the Vishnu temple of Diddasvamin;

the towns of Diddapura (location unknown); Kankanapura (perhaps modern-day Kangan village on the right bank of the Sindh River); and Didda Matha or Diddamar (another town).

Kalhana notes that in all she made 64 different foundations. Didda encased the temples that had faced damage in stronger stone walls to keep them from further harm. During her time as Queen, she even built homes for travellers who came from other parts of India (mostly central).

It would be an understatement to say it was a bad time for Kashmir's kings. Nandigupta fell ill and died within the year. So Didda made his brother Tribhuvana, her second grandson, the king. He, too, fell sick and died in another two years.

Rumours of Didda using witchcraft to kill the last two kings—her own grandsons—began to float in the kingdom. For ages, witchcraft has made its way into stories where women are in the centre. This was no exception. In fact, the historian Kalhana even notes in his records that the deaths were because of witchcraft.[8]

The last of her grandsons was Bhimagupta. He took the throne in 975 CE. And Didda was at his side just as she was for the kings who came before him.

It was around this time that Tunga, a herder of buffaloes from modern-day Poonch, came into the

---

[8]Ibid.

kingdom. He soon gained employment as a messenger and crossed paths with Didda who immediately took a liking to him. Much to the angst of many, especially since Didda was over the age of 50 when she met Tunga, the two apparently became paramours.

Perhaps these actions caused Bhimagupta to question Didda. She had him thrown into prison, where he eventually died. Following this, Didda took the throne for herself and went on to rule for 23 years. It must be noted that Didda had, in actuality, ruled over Kashmir ever since the death of her husband. Some would argue and say that it was actually even before that.

The events following Bhimagupta's removal from the throne only made Didda's rule formal. As Kalhana mentions, 'Those treacherous ministers who for sixty years had robbed sixteen kings, from King Gopala to Abhimanyu, of their dignity, lives and riches, were quickly exterminated by the energy of Queen Didda.'[9]

Tunga had now been raised to the level of Didda's chief minister, angering many at the court for obvious reasons. But Tunga managed to stop the rebellions against them, as a trusted aide of the Queen.

Didda is likely to have understood that there needed to be a clear line of succession to avoid any wars. She looked to her own family for heirs to take under her wing. She had many nephews, so she must have decided

[9]Ibid.

to see if she could find one among them worthy of Kashmir's throne.

According to one oral story, she is said to have assembled all the children before her. When they gathered in her presence, the Queen threw apples in front of them and challenged them to see who could get hold of the greatest number of apples. A fight ensued as the boys began to jostle. By the time things quietened down, many princes were holding apples. However, most of the apples were in the possession of Samgramaraja (her brother Udayaraja's son).

'How did you get so many?' she is supposed to have asked the boy. Samgramaraja replied by saying that he got the others to fight among themselves. He stayed out of the fight, thus ensuring that he was unhurt while others ended up wounded. The choice was clear—the young prince's calm mind and powers of reasoning, even while under duress, was exactly what the throne needed. Thus began another chapter in the history of Kashmir as Didda passed on the crown of the Lohara dynasty.

Mahmud of Ghazni tried to attack Kashmir twice under Didda's nephew Samgramaraja's reign. The Sultan from Afghanistan had to accept defeat both times and retreat to his home country because of the strong military and kingdom that Didda had left behind, and the able successor she had chosen.

By passing on Kashmir's crown to her brother's son, Didda established a new direction and line of succession for Kashmir's throne. In an alternate reality, Kshemagupta's family would have ruled over Kashmir.

A few historians have been particularly cruel to Didda, perhaps because they looked at her life only from the male gaze. The roots of patriarchy were sown far before Didda was even born, and every generation of women has suffered the worst of it. Didda was no exception to it.

∽

Didda is accused by many of being 'sinister' for the bloodshed her regime saw. This adjective has not been used to describe her male counterparts who have similar histories. Another queen who didn't shy from defending her throne was Rani Karnavati of Garhwal, the woman who defeated Shah Jahan's forces. She is said to have allowed the enemy soldiers to return but only after chopping off their noses. Despite this act of open defiance towards Shah Jahan, this queen's story—like in Didda's case—remains restricted to their places of origin.

According to M.A. Stein: 'The statesmanlike instinct and political ability which we must ascribe to Didda in spite of all the defects of her character, are attested by the fact that she remained to the last in peaceful possession of the Kashmir throne, and was able to bequeath it to her family in undisputed possession.'[10] Even after being

[10]Stein, M.A., *Kalhana's Rajatarangini: A Chronicle of the Kings of Kashmir,*

married for only eight years, Didda left such an impression on Kashmir's history that her husband's name—and the names of the kings who immediately followed him—pale in comparison to her.

Didda is believed to have built many temples during her time. Besides those in memory of her son Abhimanyu, there was even one dedicated to Valaga—the woman who brought her up and carried her around.

The unfounded suspicions of witchcraft floated only because of her gender. Ambition and brutal practicality—the attributes that history so greatly admires in male monarchs—are considered by many to be Didda's faults. Conquerors and rulers are famed for their 'everything is fair in love and war' approach but only if they are men.

As a polarizing personality, Didda is both loved and reviled by those who know her story. But in death as in life, it is unlikely that Didda would be bothered by the thoughts of a few. One only hopes more people could have discovered and impartially documented the story of this enigmatic Queen, who invoked strong devotion in those who had the chance to know her. Didda outlived kings and queens, ministers of the court, as well as her own son and many grandsons. The Lohara dynasty, which Didda helped build, lasted till 1320.

She dominated life in and outside the court in Kashmir for a little over half a century. By the time the

---

Motilal Banarsidass, 2017.

sun set on her life and rule, she was well into her late 70s. When Didda died in 1003, she left behind a story shaped by a childhood spent being treated differently. What remains of Didda's legacy is a residential locality, Diddamar, on the right bank of the ever-flowing waters of the Jhelum.

If you ever find yourself walking along the banks of the cold waters of the Jhelum, dear reader, or gaze upon the old walls of a temple built a long time ago—think of the Queen who was often marked out for her limp. Remember how Didda charted her own destiny, walked her own path and rose above what others thought she could and could not do.

Noor

The Spirit of Resistance

DACHAU, 1944

As the train slowly pulled into the station, the calm inside it was at odds with the events unfolding outside. The sound of bombs shook the ground not very far away. Inside the train car, four women sat together by the window. They were being escorted by guards, and everyone else on the train steered clear of this group.

The Allied forces—comprising soldiers from France, Poland and Britain—had landed on the coasts of Normandy in France about three months ago. These troops had come to reclaim the territories usurped by the Axis Powers. Their arrival, as we know, changed the history of mankind. Perhaps, if they had come sooner, the fate of these women would have been different.

The Germans who were escorting these women kept a strict watch on them. The women, knowing their fate was sealed for good, talked without care. They spoke in English at a time and place where it was frowned upon.

Having changed multiple trains, the women then walked 2 km to Dachau. One of the first Nazi concentration camps, this was opened shortly after Hitler became Germany's Chancellor. Dachau was meant for political prisoners.

The women had handcuffs on and were expected to go through the iron gate with '*Arbeit macht frei*' inscribed on it; translated from German, these words meant 'work sets you free'.

The women had a fair idea of what this 'place of work' actually was. It was a torture camp. People were forced to work in inhumane conditions and they had no rights whatsoever. The very look of the place, with its harsh searchlights and high walls lined with barbed wire, screamed how horrific the place truly was. But what really went on behind these gates was unknown to much of the world. Only rumours existed, taking on forms so strange that one cannot distinguish the factual from the unreal. Only later did the world realize that these camps were as agonizing as they had heard, if not more.

Over a period of 12 years, close to 2 lakh people were put in this camp.[1] At times, the families and friends of the people brought here as prisoners did not even know where their loved ones were being taken. It was hard not to lose hope once you crossed these gates—hard to believe this was not a nightmare once you saw the people crammed together, half-naked and starving to the point of their bones showing.

New prisoners, like these women, knew this would be their fate. They also knew there was another possibility here, death. Historians went on to record over 40,000 deaths in this camp alone.[2] The actual list of those dead still remains unknown.

The women were separated soon after they entered the gates. Three of them were taken away together and the fourth, a smallish person labelled 'a very dangerous prisoner', remained alone in a cell.[3] As dusk turned to night, this lone woman realized she would never see her travel companions again. Not

---

[1]'Dachau', *Holocaust Encyclopedia, United States Holocaust Memorial Museum,* https://tinyurl.com/45zvjz57. Accessed on 30 April 2023.
[2]Ibid.
[3]Basu, Shrabani, *Spy Princess: The Life of Noor Inayat Khan,* Lotus Collection, 2006.

that she had much time to wonder about them for the guards took turns slapping her around. They kicked her over and over again, till she tasted dust.

It must have been difficult for her to understand how she found herself in these circumstances. Her life, as envisioned by her family, was in a world far removed from the fear and violence that the last few weeks of her life had so freely showered on her.

According to various oral accounts, she didn't have a mean or violent bone in her body. She was a poet and writer who grew up in a Sufi household; a soft-spoken person who loved music. And by virtue of being a descendant of Tipu Sultan, the Tiger of Mysore, this woman was a princess with Indian blood. She was Noor Inayat Khan.

NOOR'S STORY

After winning three wars against the British, Tipu Sultan—who ruled the kingdom of Mysore between the years of 1782 and 1799—lost the fourth of these bloody battles. The control of his territories in South India slipped into the hands of the EIC. Tipu Sultan was killed in that battle. His children were banished to Vellore (in modern-day Tamil Nadu).[4]

---

[4]Raja, Siddharth, 'Tipu Sultan: The Forgotten Connection with India's

Every now and then, the Sultan's sons would try to revolt against the British who had banished them and they would be imprisoned. Even as the turmoil between the two factions simmered on a slow burner, Tipu Sultan's family went into hiding. The Sultan's surviving family was only spoken about in whispers, lest the British get a whiff of their whereabouts. Their mere existence was a threat to the vice-like grip that the British had on the country. The British had come to India for trade and stayed back to exploit India's bountiful riches and resources. Native kings, queens and citizens with independent minds were the only obstacles in their path.

That is why very few people knew of the existence of Qasim Bibi, the Sultan's granddaughter. When the capital of Tipu Sultan's kingdom, Srirangapatna (in modern-day Karnataka), fell after his death, Qasim Bibi was whisked away by two men still loyal to the Sultan. She was only 14 then. No one should ever know about who she was, the girl was told.[5]

Despite the rigidness that her new life offered, the old and uncompromising rules of courtship still applied to her. Since she was of royal blood, Qasim Bibi was only permitted to wed a person who had some noble standing.

First Sepoy Mutiny', *The Wire*, 10 November 2018, https://tinyurl.com/3nfanhah. Accessed 23 June 2023.

[5]Sharma, Unnati, 'World War 2 Spy Noor Inayat Khan First Indian Origin Woman to Get UK Memorial Plaque', *The Print*, 28 August 2020, https://tinyurl.com/2b9sk6cc. Accessed on 25 June 2023.

The secret life that Qasim Bibi lived was set to shift in 1860, when the then Maharaja of Mysore (now Mysuru) organized a music tournament. This event saw people from far and wide pouring into the kingdom. Among these musicians was Maula Bakhsh, a strapping young man by all accounts.

Trained in both North Indian classical music as well as the South Indian Carnatic form, Maula Bakhsh also played the rudra veena. His openness to experiment with music endeared him to Maharaja Sayajirao Gaekwad III.

Maula Bakhsh won the competition in Mysore with ease. And the Maharaja of Mysore was so pleased that he granted Maula Bakhsh several distinctive honours. Among other things, he gave him a turban and a turban ornament; a large umbrella; and the right to have an attendant announce his presence when he walked into a room.[6] Maula Bakhsh was from a family of zamindars. The honours bestowed on him by Mysore's Maharaja were signs to mark royalty. Maula Bakhsh's flair for music raised his rank to nobility.

Convinced that the musician had a bright future ahead of him, Princess Qasim Bibi's guardians offered him her hand in marriage. They told him the secret of her ancestry. The two were wed shortly after that. They moved to Baroda (now Vadodara)—on the invitation

---

[6]Basu, Shrabani, *Spy Princess: The Life of Noor Inayat Khan*, Lotus Collection, 2006.

of the kingdom's ruler Maharaja Sayajirao Gaekwad III. Along with the Maharaja, they went on to establish the Gyanshala—a place to learn music which still exists. It's called the Faculty of Performing Arts today.[7]

Their family flourished here. In 1882, the couple welcomed a grandson whom they named Hazrat Inayat Khan. This boy went on to excel in poetry as well as music. Eventually, it was realized that his true calling was a spiritual one.

Inayat Khan grew up to be a music teacher but perhaps his greatest contribution to the world is his work to promote Universal Sufism—a faith that teaches one to treat all religions as rays of light from the same sun. His ideas particularly echoed and gained popularity in the West.

Inayat Khan left India to promote Sufism in 1910. He met his future wife, an American woman called Ora Ray Baker, while delivering a lecture at the Ramakrishna Mission Ashram in San Francisco. After some resistance from both sides of the family, the two finally married in 1913. Many in the Sufi order today know of the American Ora Baker as Ameena Begum, a devout Sufi practitioner.

After living in London for a while, the couple then moved to Moscow. It was there, on New Year's Day 1914, that Ameena Begum gave birth to the first of their children. They called her Babuli at home. To the

---

[7]Ibid.

world outside, she was Noor-un-nissa (meaning the 'light of womanhood'). Much of Noor's stories comes to us through the works of writers like Shrabani Basu, as well as those who would go on to be Noor's friends later in life, like Jean Overton Fuller.

∽

The years around Noor's birth were marked with international tension. People were worried that their respective countries might actually go to war. This fear was not unfounded. Soon it became clear to everyone that a muddle of international political alliances had failed. There was going to be war. This war went down in history as the First World War.

Just like others, Noor's parents had also been concerned about the eventuality of war. So shortly before the beginning of the First World War, the family decided it was best to leave Russia. They set sail for their former home, hoping their young family would be safe in London.

They spent the next few years in Bloomsbury, where Noor is believed to have spent hours in the garden. Folk tales had taught her that a world of magic existed tucked just out of sight; as a child, she would look under the garden flowers for fairies and woodland creatures. Noor's playmates included her beloved siblings: Vilayat (born in 1916); Hidayat (1917); and Khair-un-nissa or Claire

(1919). Except Noor, all of Inayat Khan's children were born in England.

Times were hard for almost everyone after the First World War and things were no different for Noor's family. Sometimes they didn't even have enough to eat. It was in this set up of a close-knit family that Noor's brother Vilayat became one of her closest friends.[8]

Some believe that a child's behaviour in early life is a good indicator for how and who they are going to grow up to be. If that's the case, then a lifetime of Noor's actions can be distilled into one incident. When Noor was about four, she would demand chocolates from the adults around her. It was ordinary for a child to want chocolates, so no one thought much of it. Then, one day, her family discovered that Noor had not been eating any of the chocolates. All of them were in a box in her room, still unopened. They lay in that box like tiny pieces of treasure wrapped in bright and colourful paper. Noor had apparently heard that the children in Russia were going hungry because the war had soaked up so many resources and livelihoods. This hurt her so much that she had been collecting chocolates to send to them.

By the time the First World War came to an end, things had become harder for Noor's family in many ways. They were not doing very well financially. On top of that, the

---

[8]Ibid.

British government continued to actively watch them since Inayat Khan had come in touch with many of the leaders involved in India's fight for independence (including Mahatma Gandhi and Sarojini Naidu). On the advice of their friends, Noor's family decided to make a journey across the waters again. This time they went to France.

In 1920, the family put down roots in Suresnes (a few kilometres from the heart of Paris). Their house was called 'Fazal Manzil', or 'the House of Blessing'. They settled into their new life well, especially with the children picking up French. By this time, Inayat Khan had established himself as a Sufi leader and poet.

A few years later, in 1927, Inayat Khan planned a solo trip to India. While in his country of birth, Inayat Khan was struck by pneumonia. He was visiting his grandfather Maula Bakhsh's house when he fell deathly ill. He passed away there.

His body was laid to rest near the Dargah Sharif of Hazrat Khwaja Nizamuddin Aulia in Delhi. After his family got the news, his grief-stricken wife and children prepared to travel across the ocean to visit his grave. It was this unfortunate event—the passing of her father—that brought Noor to the land of her ancestors for the very first time. The family stayed in India for a few months before returning to France.

Her husband's passing had a lasting impact on Ameena Begum. She retreated from everything and everyone, choosing to spend her time alone. As the eldest child, the responsibilities of the house fell on Noor's young shoulders. She was 13 at the time.

Noor directed all her focus on two things alone—her education and her siblings. She spent much of her adult life in France, studying child psychology at the University of Sorbonne. Following the tradition of her ancestors, Noor also studied music. She also composed music for the harp and piano. She took lessons at the Paris Conservatory under the leading French composer and music teacher Juliette Nadia Boulanger.

Among the most famous pictures of Noor is one in which she is sitting calm and composed, almost as if she were a painting. There is a white veil on her head and a veena in her hands. Oral stories indicate that the veena was popularized by her father in the West, long before musicians such as Ravi Shankar and George Harrison roped in new audiences for Indian classical music.

The girl who once looked for fairies among the flowers grew up to be a fine writer. Her short stories were lined with creatures of magic and mystique, as well as Indian icons such as Meera Bai. She wrote with ease in both English as well as in French, and wrote a lot of stories for children. These stories appeared on the French radio and in children's magazines. Noor also published a collection titled *Twenty Jataka Tales*, a collection of stories based on the teachings of the Buddha. Tortoises, monkeys and birds of different kinds are some of the characters from this well-loved book.[9]

While all the Khan siblings played at least two instruments, the daughters were particularly encouraged to develop their talents. Maybe this was done in the hope that it could help find them good husbands. It was assumed that both Noor and Claire would marry rich Indian men and that being accomplished in socially respected disciplines, such as music, would give them a higher standing.

However, Noor had other plans for herself. She fell in love with a fellow music student, a Turkish Jew. There was strong disapproval from their families, yet the relationship lasted for six years. The relationship ended, but it made Noor aware of the worrying plight of Jews in Europe as Hitler's powers continued to grow.

∽

By this time, nations were on the brink of the Second World War and life had become uncertain again. Both Noor and her sister signed up with the French Red Cross to train as nurses. And when the war came knocking, they continued to work at the hospital they were placed at till the whole city was evacuated. When news of enemy soldiers nearing the main cities broke, even hospitals were evacuated. Things got so bad that once again, after

---

[9]Khan, Noor Inayat, *Twenty Jataka Tales*, East-West Publications Fonds, 1985.

building a new life from scratch, the family realized it was best to move again. They decided to go back to England.

According to Shrabani Basu's book, while they were waiting to leave France, Noor and her sister decided they wanted to keep working with the Red Cross. But owing to bureaucratic hurdles, the sisters were told that they would need certificates from their unit if they wanted to continue working after they left the place. They did not really have a choice, so they travelled 200 miles to get the proper documentation. When they arrived at the address they had been given, they found that the place had already been emptied out. The journey had been for nothing. In the middle of all this running around, a French policeman got hold of Noor's passport. It stated that she was born in Moscow. Suspecting that she was a spy, both Noor and Claire ended up spending a night in jail till the policeman got confirmation of their innocence. As the saying goes, 'bad news comes in threes'. The third blow came in the form of news that Paris had fallen. German tanks now patrolled the streets they had once dearly loved. The French tricolour had now been replaced by the Nazi swastika. The world found itself completely engulfed in the Second World War. As German troops continued to advance into France, Noor and her family fled to the port city of Bordeaux. From there, they set sail and reached England in June 1940.

It is in the darkest of times that sometimes one finds friends. Noor found one such friend in Jean Overton

Fuller, a young woman who lived near Noor's house during the family's second stint in England. Jean went on to write Noor's biography later. By August 1940, people had begun to experience the full effects of the Second World War in London too.

More and more people around Noor and her family were donning the uniform to fight the Nazis. Noor and her siblings were pacifists. They had, after all, grown up in a home where any form of violence was discouraged thanks to their parents' Sufi leanings.

So how does a woman who denounces violence and writes stories for children land up in a Nazi concentration camp? The regular broadcasts about the war over radio, and the dispatches from the war-torn areas moved Noor. Perhaps it was the fall of Paris, a city she had grown up in that stirred something in her. Despite the objections she had towards war, like her brother Vilayat, Noor realized that she could not just wait by the sidelines.

A little while after the Nazis marched into Poland, Noor and Vilayat had a long conversation. Despite their commitment to non-violence, they were now facing a situation that challenged the ideals they had grown up with. Writer Shrabani Basu points out in *Spy Princess* that Noor, who had read the Bhagavad Gita alongside Islamic texts, must have remembered the saying 'action is better than inaction' during these troubled times.

She must have seen advertisements asking men to sign up everywhere and felt the need to do something concrete. One example of how the contribution of women has been pushed to the sidelines of history is how little the world knows about the Night Witches.[10] That is the name given by the German soldiers to the all-women Soviet Union pilot squad. Till the end of the Second World War, these female combat units would fly at night and just let their engines idle. They would glide to the point where they were to drop bombs. The Germans felt that the sound of them gliding through the air resembled the sound of broomsticks being used. And that is how the Night Witches got their name.

Noor managed to acquire her Red Cross certificate. Vilayat joined the Royal Air Force (RAF), but Noor's application for the Women's Auxiliary Air Force (WAAF) was denied. This was all because her birth certificate said that she was born in Moscow.

Giving it a try would have been enough for some, but the gentle Noor had a rather persistent streak. She sent in a complaint to the concerned ministry saying that, irrespective of where she was born, she should be able to serve her country.[11] Shortly after this, Noor received both an apology and an appointment letter.

As one of the people who interviewed her before she was recruited recalls, even after the memory of

---

[10]Garber, Megan, 'Night Witches: The Female Fighter Pilots of World War II', *The Atlantic,* 15 July 2013, https://tinyurl.com/p742h9d7. Accessed on 30 April 2023.

[11]Basu, Shrabani, *Spy Princess: The Life of Noor Inayat Khan,* Lotus, 2006.

the other candidates faded, he remembered Noor. He remembered her still features, her soft voice and the fine spirit glowing in her.[12]

On 19 November 1940, Noor joined the WAAF as Nora Inayat Khan. Her name, a coming together of her mother's maiden name Ora and her own name, was created to avoid complications.

Nora would be easier than 'Noor' for her English companions. Some also came to know of her as Nora Baker, with her mother's maiden name. She even had to get her religious affiliation registered to the Church of England because she was told that was easier. Since she had been brought up in a home where all religions were equal, maybe ticking a box on some paper did not mean a great deal to Noor.

Noor then began her training to operate wireless communication equipment. This was WAAF's first batch of radio officers. After many rounds of training, Noor's supervisors realized she was among the best they had. Her assessment reports were always among the best and she seemed determined to accomplish anything she set her sights on. Well, almost! The people who trained with her remembered her as a gentle soul; someone with extraordinary beauty. But they also remembered her being a bad dancer.[13] She never did master the art of

---

[12]Fuller, Jean Overton, *Noor-un-nisa Inayat Khan (Madeleine)*, East-West Publications Fonds, 1971.
[13]Ibid.

dance, but then dancing was of no use or interest to her.

She was later recruited to join the Special Operations Executive (SOE), a secret British organization, during the Second World War. Three secret departments had come together to form this organization and their task was to carry out secret missions in occupied Europe. Some even call this department 'Churchill's Secret Army' (after Winston Churchill, then the prime minister of Britain).

One thing that worried Noor's seniors at SOE was that she seemed to be a bad match for what they were training her to do. The air of innocence she had was not a show she put on. Noor had spent much of her life in acts of meditation, pursuing music and writing stories with moral themes. Now it seemed like she was incapable of lying. She was kept there because of her skills alone.

During her training days, Noor also worked with Leo Marks (one of Britain's top codemakers). In his book about codemakers in the Second World War (*Between Silk and Cyanide: A Codemaker's War, 1941–1945*), Marks recounted the time spent with Noor. He recalled how she had made fewer mistakes than the other trainees but her mistakes were 'inventive'. Marks realized he could help her polish her skills by linking the work she had to do with a subject she was passionate about. He told her the animal stories she loved so dearly from *Twenty Jataka Tales* could help her become an excellent coder. Once, using an example featuring monkeys, he suggested that she think of the letters in a code as monkeys trying to cross a bridge that stretched all the way from Paris to London. If she didn't guide the monkeys one by one methodically and with care, giving each one of them her individual attention, her monkey friends could get spotted and shot. A badly written code, he said, was akin to lying. When Noor re-attempted the coding after that, it was perfect. [14]

Noor's child-like nature was seen in her interactions with him as well. According to Marks, shortly after they spoke about monkeys, she asked him if it was okay to sometimes replace the monkeys with pigs instead. Marks understood the reference. One of the stories she had written was about two pigs, named Mahatundila and Cullatindila.

Noor also did some advanced training at Abingdon where she mastered the art of sending and receiving messages. Except for a few people, no one knew that this shy woman was an Indian princess and a writer whose father was one of the beacons of Sufism. Noor always kept a low profile.

She had also become politically conscious by now, and was following the developments in the Indian Independence movement. Her seniors had always felt that one could not really predict Noor's actions, and one example of this presented itself when she had to appear

---

[14]Marks, Leo, *Between Silk and Cyanide: A Codemaker's War, 1941–1945*, Free Press, 2001.

before a commission. This commission was to decide whether or not Noor could participate in the war efforts.

Noor knew this was a delicate opportunity but couldn't keep her personal beliefs aside when asked. She explained to this council, a group of people loyal to the British Crown, that she was in favour of India's independence. She went on to talk about how Indians should play a larger part in the war internationally, and also be able to defend themselves back in India. The panel questioning her did not expect any of this. They had not realized that Noor had signed up to fight for a cause and not just for a nation. This was her way of opposing authoritarianism.

According to her, India needed to be free of Britain's rule. And perhaps after the Second World War was over, Noor told the panel, she'd even consider fighting for India's cause. She expressed a desire to help better communication between Britain and India. She said this despite knowing these views were not favoured by the British government at all.

Vilayat had by then joined the Navy. After what happened with the panel, Noor began to lose hope that she would get commissioned because of her frankness.

It is likely she realized she couldn't do much in the meantime, so she continued perfecting her Morse code. She refused to let worrying distract her from what she was there for. Maybe she was focussed on the task at hand, so as to not let worry distract her. Noor's linguistic qualifications and radio skills had caught the commission's eye. Noor—who spoke English, French and Hindi—was now being sought out for a life she had never even considered. She was about to become a secret field agent. Hers was a strange, strange life—especially for those who didn't know Noor personally. This young woman—born in Moscow to Indian and American parents—was now going to be in service for Britain. Here was a woman who had always distanced herself from violence and lies, but now she was embarking on a journey lined with secrecy, betrayal and violence—the markers of the life of a spy.

By the time Noor was ready to be posted overseas she was an expert in Morse code. She had also become familiar with interrogation methods the enemy might use if she were ever taken prisoner. This included being stripped in front of the enemy, and being made to repeat her cover story multiple times. She also had to memorize the names and faces of German and French officials who had chosen to side with Hitler.

Heavily influenced by the strides that Indians were making back home with the Quit India Movement, Noor said: 'I wish some Indians would win high military distinction in this war. If one or two could do something in the Allied service which was very brave and which everybody admired, it would help to make a bridge between the English people and the Indians.'[15] No one could have

[15]Rachel, Hannah, 'Noor Inayat, Indian-Origin Spy Who Could

predicted that Noor would have the rare distinction of being one of these people. One morning in June 1943, Noor bid goodbye to her friend Jean, telling her that she was going abroad. Jean found this strange but did not press for details.[16] Days after that Noor was flown to occupied France. On 16 June 1943, she was dropped off in a valley near Angers and she made her way to Paris from there. In her new home in Paris, she was to be Jeanne-Marie Renier, a children's nurse. Her code name was Madeleine. She was the first female wireless radio operator to be flown into occupied France. Here, among other things, she was to aid the French Resistance.

According to Shrabani Basu, the life of a spy did not come easily to Noor. Even though she was one of the best that her trainers had seen, leading a double life did not come naturally to her. This meant that Noor was vulnerable to making mistakes—the smallest of which could cost her dearly. One time, while making tea for a room full of people, she poured out the milk in teacups and then topped it off with tea. This was not how they usually made tea there. Even a small mistake like this could have raised suspicions about Noor's identity.

In the days that followed, Noor continued to learn how different it was being in training and how real the

---

Feature on Britain's £50 Note', *The Week*, 23 October 2018, https://tinyurl.com/8732bkzy. Accessed on 30 April 2023.

[16]Fuller, Jean Overton, *Noor-un-nisa Inayat Khan (Madeleine)*, East-West Publications Fonds, 1971.

danger was when one was in the field. No one, not even the people back home in the London office, knew that the French Resistance was in serious trouble. People suspected of being spies were already getting arrested. The French Resistance was beginning to fall apart in Paris. Instructions meant to keep agents safe were ignored by a few, but many were about to pay a hefty price for it.

Records suggest that it was Noor who informed the headquarters that an entire circuit of spies had been exposed. She had to be the bearer of bad news of how the Gestapo (the German secret police) had arrested hundreds of people. They had even arrested farmers on whose lands radio equipment, mounted on parachutes, had landed. Many of these people broke down under torture to reveal the identity and whereabouts of their contacts. After this, those who had not been arrested had to flee. This series of unfortunate events meant that Noor was the only one left in Paris who could send a message back home.[17]

Noor was asked by her bosses to leave Paris after all this. Her mission of sending reports from the ground about what the Resistance needed—forged identity papers, arms, etc.—and what the Germans were planning, would have to stop because the Germans were now also looking for radio operators. They were using vans equipped with

---

[17]Basu, Shrabani, *Spy Princess: The Life of Noor Inayat Khan*, Lotus Collections, 2006.

technology capable of detecting radio transmissions. They could also trace radio signals and figure out where it was sent from. Any day a van could turn up in front of Noor and arrest her. It took one of these vans just about 20 minutes to trace a signal. However, Noor refused to leave. According to a report of *The London Gazette* (April 1949):

> During the weeks immediately following her arrival, the Gestapo made mass arrests in the Paris Resistance groups to which she had been detailed. She refused however to abandon what had become the principal and most dangerous post in France, although given the opportunity to return to England, because she did not wish to leave her French comrades without communications and she hoped also to rebuild her group.[18]

According to Shrabani Basu, those who had trained her back in England expressed serious concerns about how Noor would be able to survive in the field. She was not street smart. But what worried them even more was Noor's utter distaste of lying. They had all considered her to be too feminine, soft and gentle. Moreover, the emotional Noor usually made strong attachments. The only reason they sent her on the mission was because they desperately needed to send people and Noor was good at what she

---

[18]'Supplement to The London Gazette of Friday 1 April 1949', *The Gazette*, 5 April 1949, https://tinyurl.com/3ajswpxc. Accessed on 30 April 2023.

did. It is ironic that Noor, who at one point was the only link Paris had with London, was almost not even sent into France.

Noor knew how difficult things were in Paris after she had to do the work of multiple radio operators because of the crackdown. Almost as if to make things harder, all her equipment was packed into a heavy suitcase that she had to lug around with her. The only way for her to stay safe in a place rife with secret police was to always be on the move. By doing so, she could avoid the Germans from pinpointing where the coded transmissions were coming from. Sometimes, in between messages about developments on the ground, Noor would also pass on messages to her family (particularly to Vilayat). These messages were always in code.

Her family got these messages, but they did not know where Noor was or what she was doing. Neither side knew that someone else had also been reading Noor's messages. They had a double agent in their midst, who was making copies of Noor's messages and then passing them to the London office. This is how the Germans were certain there was still a radio operator in Paris.

Even the people in her London circuit did not know her real name. This meant that her identity could not be easily compromised. Even the people who knew that her codename was Madeline were under the impression that her real name was Nora.

As Shrabani Basu notes in Noor's biography, she had

a rather close call one time. This was when she had to send an urgent message to London. Instead of venturing out, Noor hung her radio antenna from a tree right outside her apartment. The sun had long set and this is why Noor thought no one would take notice of her antenna. Well, someone did! It was a German officer who stayed in the same building as Noor.

When this officer found Noor fixing the antenna, he asked if she needed any assistance. Since Noor spoke and dressed as a French woman, it was easy to assume that she was French. Presumably, the officer thought Noor just wanted a better signal to listen to music on the radio. No one would immediately assume that a spy was living in the same building as government officers.

It was for this reason that Noor moved around so frequently. Old neighbours and people she lived alongside (when her own family still lived in France) became the people she visited while on a job.

Noor knew many of her contacts had been flushed out and jailed; some were even executed. This was why she started working with the people she knew from before the Second World War, so that she could distance herself from people who might have been compromised. When Noor went to her old contacts, they welcomed her with open arms. By then, Noor had developed a system where she would sit anywhere to transmit her messages—rooftops, near windows and in cars parked in alley ways. This ensured that no transmission could be traced to a single place.

Once 30 airmen from the Allied forces, who were shot down in France, were able to safely escape with Noor's help. This was possible because Noor's message about the crash reached the right people at the right time.[19] This information came to light when the British government (posthumously) awarded Noor with the George Cross in April 1949. The award, given out by the United Kingdom, recognizes acts of heroism for courage shown in circumstances of extreme danger.

One day, she was instructed to meet two Canadian agents from the French Resistance at a café. Only the Germans knew that the actual agents had already been arrested. Two German officers were pretending to be the agents Noor was to meet. She would have walked into a trap if she went to the café. According to Fuller, the Germans thought they could use Noor as a pawn and trap others, just as they had used the identity of the Canadian agents to trap Noor. They managed to reach one of Noor's contacts before she realized it was all a ploy. She then had to watch as a bunch of policemen bundled her friend, and took him away.

Noor frequently changed her hair colour and overall appearance to evade the enemy. Even if the Germans knew her French name, her codename or even how she looked, they did not know where she lived. There was no

[19]Ibid.

fixed address for her because she was almost always on the move. And this was the case until a Frenchwoman walked into the Gestapo office, offering the very details they wanted. She sold Noor out for some reward money, but many believe it was out of sheer envy.

∽

Noor had been living on borrowed time ever since she landed in France. Finally, her luck ran out. People assigned to watch out for Noor spotted her walking down a street. She was smart enough to shake them off. But when she reached home, another officer was waiting for her. A violent struggle ensued; Noor even bit him hard enough to draw blood before he managed to cuff her at gunpoint. In *Madeleine*, Fuller writes that the officer who cuffed Noor immediately called his headquarters and asked them to send reinforcements. When this help arrived, they found the officer standing as far away from Noor as possible. Noor was still cuffed to the couch but she was clawing the air to reach Pierre. She looked like a tigress in that moment, the officers went on to say.[20] Jean's account of Noor comes largely from the conversations she had with people who met Noor, including quite a few German soldiers.

---

[20]Fuller, Jean Overton, *Noor-un-nisa Inayat Khan (Madeleine)*, East-West Publications Fonds,1971.

Strange are the ways of the world. According to Fuller, Noor had only recently agreed to go back home to London, and the Germans had caught her days before she was to leave France. The woman who was thought to be too timid and gentle to be a spy refused to go down easily. She even attempted to escape the Germans twice after being taken into custody. And though her escape plan was foiled, her captors could not get Noor to betray any of her friends. They could not even get her to tell them her real name.

In a bid to get Noor to crack, they showed her the letters that they had copied and kept through their double agent. Even that did not do the trick, and Noor attempted to escape again.

It was, perhaps, because of this unbreakable spirit that Noor was labelled a 'very dangerous prisoner'. She was beaten up and kept in solitary confinement. Both tactics failed to break her. It is almost surreal to think that such a gentle woman evaded the enemy for so long; even after being captured, her presence kept them on guard. Imprisoned without any contact from the world, Noor had no way to track the passing days. Her only human connection was when she was given food. Even then, the people sent in to give her food were instructed not to talk to her.

The Germans continued to transmit messages to London pretending to be Noor, while she languished in the Pforzheim Prison. London did not know she had been caught for a long time. Down the hall from her cell were three other women. They suspected there was another person being held there, and realized later this prisoner was always kept alone and shackled. They later came to know her as Nora Baker.

One of the women managed to scratch a message in her tin food bowl using the knitting needles they were given to keep themselves occupied. When Noor got the bowl, she replied with a message of her own. This way, miles away from home—in a prison where she could not see or hear anyone except her captors—Noor found friends.

One of these women was a French national called Yolande Lagrave. Yolande had been sent to the Pforzheim Prison in early 1944, about two months after Noor was taken to the same prison. The two managed to exchange addresses in the hope that they could contact each other if they survived. According to Shrabani Basu, Yolande wrote down Noor's addresses on a piece of paper that she managed to sew into the helm of her skirt.

Unlike Noor, the others were allowed to hear of the developments in the world outside. If Noor ever heard anything, it was only through the limited communication she had with these women.

Noor had been there for so long that she had also managed to make friends with other prisoners—two of whom would sing the news to her. But, for this act of insolence—of interacting with others—Noor was beaten up. Noor's response to this was to meditate. She was deeply unhappy, and no one who survived the war challenges that, but she would still try and cheer the other prisoners when she could—urging them to have faith.

On the day of America's Independence for instance, Noor's message on her bowl read 'Here's to the Fourth of July', in French. On 14 July, Bastille Day, she wrote 'Long live free France, for that keeps us together.'[21] She also managed to add two flags—one English and the other French—on the tin. In the darkest of times, it is the smallest ray of strength that can make the heart hope. In the words of Vilayat, 'One is never so strong as when one is broken.'[22]

Sometime in September 1944, Noor inscribed her last message to Yolande before she was moved from the prison. Yolande continued to stay there till the Allies came and liberated the prisoners on 1 May 1945.

Immediately after she was freed, Yolande began to write to the addresses Noor had given her. But no one had heard from Noor. No messages bearing any of her aliases had been received. Records suggest that Noor was moved from Pforzheim on 11 September 1944 to the office of the Gestapo in Karlsruhe—a place that has since become infamous for the ill treatment and killing of British agents from the French section. This is exactly

---

[21]Fuller, Jean Overton, *Noor-un-nisa Inayat Khan (Madeleine)*, East-West Publications Fonds, 1971.

[22]Khan, Pir Vilayat Inayat, *Thinking Like the Universe: The Sufi Path of Awakening*, Thorsons, 2000.

the criteria that Noor met.

At Karlsruhe she was joined by three other female prisoners, one of whom Noor knew from her training days. From there, they went to the train station at Stuttgart and were then put on a train to Munich. The men accompanying them made them sit next to windows so that they could not attempt to escape.

Just out of her long-drawn solitary confinement, Noor freely chatted with other women. One can only imagine that it would have been a surreal moment. Even if the women did not know where they were going, they must have known that it wasn't going to be a good place. They were headed to the Dachau concentration camp, as mentioned earlier. This would be the last journey they would ever make.

Once inside the camp, the women travelling with Noor were taken aside and shot. Noor was singled out here too, for the 'dangerous' woman she was supposed to be. Here, to break her spirit her captors stripped her and beat her till their own limbs ached. Several accounts suggest that these beatings went on for the whole night.

The exact sequence of events of 12 and 13 September 1944—the time during which Noor was tortured at Dachau—are unclear. But all records confirm excessive violence. In the early hours of the next day, Noor was ordered to get on her knees. Her captor then put his pistol to her head and pulled the trigger. Noor only had one word to say before she was shot—'Liberte'.[23]

Another account of the story says that Noor was burned alive in the crematorium at the concentration camp. The details continue to shift and vary in the several retellings of Noor's story.

∽

In October 1944, the London office sent word to her family that they had lost touch with Noor. Right up till then, Noor's mother did not even know the battles Noor had been fighting and the sacrifice she had made. On 4 October 1945, it was recommended that Noor be appointed a Member of the Order of the British Empire (MBE) in recognition of her bravery and devotion. Everyone continued to assume that Noor was missing. It was only in April 1946 that Noor's officer-in-charge, Vera May Atkins, began to receive details of Noor's death. A little while later, Vilayat also received a letter from Yolande, the French woman who had promised to find Noor after the war. Fuller mentions in her book that Vilayat and Jean met Vera personally at Vera's apartment in November 1949 to talk about Noor's whereabouts. As explained in Fuller's book, Vera had been tasked to track down her now-defunct department's missing agents.

---

[23]Basu, Shrabani, *Spy Princess: The Life of Noor Inayat Khan*, Lotus Collections, 2006.

Seven months after Noor was shot, Allied troops advanced and reached Dachau. The prisoners there were freed.

Renée Garry, the woman who had sold Noor's identity to the Gestapo, was later acquitted by a French court, writes Shrabani Basu. The man who had shot Noor in Dachau was tried for war crimes and hanged in May 1946.

Shortly after the war, Fuller travelled extensively to interview the people Noor had met, both friends and enemies. She wrote a book called *Madeleine*, after Noor's code name, in 1952. It was later revised and published as *Born for Sacrifice* and *Noor-un-nisa Inayat Khan.*

Several books, including *Double Webs* and *The Starr Affair* by Jean Overton Fuller, as well as *Flames in the Field* by Rita Kramer, suggest that England understood the Gestapo was arresting agents. It is believed that despite the danger of getting caught, London knowingly continued to send agents so that the enemy would remain distracted. The Germans would then focus on finding these agents, instead of spending all their energies on stopping the Allied troops.

On 5 April 1949, Noor was posthumously awarded the George Cross. Her citation identifies her as the first woman operator to have infiltrated into enemy-occupied France.[24] Her death is recorded to have occurred on 12 September 1944. In 1946 the French awarded Noor the

---

[24]'Supplement to The London Gazette of Friday 1 April 1949', *The Gazette*, 5 April 1949, https://tinyurl.com/3ajswpxc. Accessed on 30 April 2023.

highest civilian award, the Croix de Guerre with Golden Star. She was only 30 when she died.

Her more famous ancestor, Tipu Sultan, has left behind a controversial legacy in India. While on one side, he stands accused of religious persecution and ransacking temples, on the other the Muslim ruler is also known for having high-ranking Hindu courtiers and restoring Hindu temples in his domain after the Marathas looted them.[25] Noor may have had the blood of the Tiger of Mysore in her veins, but she was much more than her ancestry.

A bronze bust of Noor has been installed at London's Gordon Square Gardens. It serves as a reminder of her personal contribution to the world. It is also a reminder of the major role played by the Asian community in Britain's history. In August 2020, Noor became the first woman of Indian origin to be commemorated with a Blue Plaque, an honour that symbolizes that the person was of immense importance and had some connection to the site where the plaque is placed. In recognition of her contribution to English history, it stands in front of her Bloomsbury home in London. Plans to feature her face on British coins are also afoot.

---

[25]Pillai, Manu S., 'Manu S Pillai Writes: Karnataka BJP Chief's Comments Ignore the Complexity of Tipu Sultan's Record', *The Indian Express*, 21 February 2023, https://tinyurl.com/4an7zkkb. Accessed on 25 June 2023.

She remains relatively unknown in India. France knows her far better. There, she is called 'Madeline of the Resistance'. On Bastille Day, the national day of France, a military band marches to her childhood home, Fazal Manzil, and plays a well-deserved tribute to the heroine. If you ever find your way to the site of the Dachau concentration camp, dear reader, walk into the Memorial Hall and look at the plaques honouring the dead. One of these plaques bears Noor's name.

Acknowledgements

Perhaps among the first to discover my love for writing was a pre-teen girl who was just beginning to discover the joys of reading herself. This was my sister, Kimy. In rummaging through my things, as siblings are wont to do, she discovered a stack of badly written prose. Her wanting to read more of it made me aware of the power of storytelling—something I had taken for granted till then.

Stories have shaped my childhood and my career in journalism. When it was finally time to write my first book, my spirited mother, Cicily, and forever thoughtful father, Col (Rtd) S.B. Puri, started planning the in which they could make the writing process as pleasant as possible. This included numerous attempts at trying to make me live with them for a few weeks so that I wouldn't have to do any chores—the bane of my existence. The lure worked, as did the home-cooked food.

And then there's my partner-in-everything, Avanish, who has joined me in all of life's craziness. I cannot begin to list the infinite ways in which he's been my rock.

This is my first book of stories. It is grounded in historical events solely because of my commissioning editor at Rupa, the lovely Saswati Bora. Clear and concise about all that was expected of me, Saswati pushed me and worked with me to rise over the few failings we had in the very beginning of this process. I would also like to thank others at Rupa, including Sagareeka Pradhan, who made this book possible.

This book rests on the shoulders of giants, historians and documentarians—both remembered and forgotten—for this work would not have been possible if not for their contributions. Where would we even be without the stories that have already been told? Our collective human history rests on the building blocks established yesterday. Some of these names appear in this book's bibliography and footnotes as well.

I would also like to thank the editors who guided me during my early days in my journalism career, especially the late Bhupesh Bhandari. Without the unfailing guidance of the editors I've had the good fortune of working with, I would only be half the writer that I am.

There are others too, close friends and complete strangers, who have helped write this book in more ways than one. For that and so much more, thank you all.

Bibliography

Adhikari, Shona, 'Razia Sultan: The First Empress of India and the Confusion over Her Burial Site', *The Asian Age*, 8 August 2019, https://tinyurl.com/4nx8fj4z. Accessed on 5 June 2023.

Aftab, Tahera, *Inscribing South Asian Muslim Women: An Annotated Bibliography & Research Guide*, Brill, 2008.

Agrawal, Purushottam, *Who Is Bharat Mata? On History, Culture and the Idea of India: Writings by and on Jawaharlal Nehru*, Speaking Tiger Publishing, 2019.

Ahmed, Rehana, and Sumita Mukherjee, *South Asian Resistances in Britain, 1858–1947*, Continuum, 2012.

Ahsan, Sadaf, 'Noor Inayat Khan, Unlikely War Hero', *The Juggernaut*, 4 January 2023, https://tinyurl.com/3b26r3d5. Accessed on 4 June 2023.

Alexander, Michael, and Sushila Anand, *Queen Victoria's Maharajah: Duleep Singh 1838–93*, Weidenfeld & Nicolson History, 2001.

Altekar, A.S., *The Position of Women in Hindu Civilization: From Prehistoric Times to the Present Day*, Motilal Banarsidass, 2016.

Anand, Anita, *Sophia: Princess, Suffragette, Revolutionary*, Bloomsbury USA, 2016.

Andrews, Maggie, and Janis Lomas, *Hidden Heroines: The Forgotten Suffragettes*, Crowood Press, 2018.

Ankit, Kumar, 'Sati: Tragedy through the Ages', *Swarajya*, 11 October 2015, https://tinyurl.com/y7wjeuh2. Accessed on 4 June 2023.

Aranha, Jovita, 'The 5 Attempts on Mahatma Gandhi's Life: Who, Why and When', *Citizens for Justice and Peace*, 31 January 2018, https://tinyurl.com/2p85cjrx.

Balabanlilar, Lisa, 'The Emperor Jahangir and the Pursuit of Pleasure', *Journal of the Royal Asiatic Society*, Vol. 19, No. 2, April 2009, pp. 173–86.

Balakrishnan, Vijayalakshmi, *Growing Up and Away: Narratives of Indian Childhoods: Memory, History, Identity*, Oxford University Press, India, 2011.

Bamzai, P.N.K., *Culture and Political History of Kashmir: Ancient Kashmir*, Vol. 1, M.D. Publications, 1994.

Bance, Peter, *Sovereign, Squire and Rebel: Maharajah Duleep Singh*, Coronet House Publishing, 2009.

Basu, Sharbani, *Spy Princess: The Life of Noor Inayat Khan*, Lotus Collections, 2006.

Bazaz, Prem Nath, *Daughters of the Vitasta: A History of Kashmiri Women from Early Times to the Present Day*, Pamposh Publications, 1959.

Begam, Gulbadan, *The Humayun Nama*, Annette S. Beveridge (trans.), Royal Asiatic Society, 1902.

Beveridge, Henry, and Bani Prashad, *Maathir-ul-umara: Being Biographies of the Muhammadan and Hindu Officers of the Timurid Sovereigns of India from 1500 to about 1780 A.D.*,

The Asiatic Society, 2003.

Beveridge, Henry, *The Akbarnama of Abul Fazl*, Low Price Publications, 2010.

Bhalla, A.S., *Royal Tombs of India: 13th to 18th Century*, Mapin, 2009.

Bhattacharya, Sanjoy, *Expunging Variola: The Control and Eradication of Smallpox in India, 1947–1977*, Orient Longman, 2006.

Bhushan, Jamila Brij, *Sultan Raziya, Her Life and Times: A Reappraisal*, Manohar Publications, 1990.

Bressler, Richard, *The Thirteenth Century: A World History*, McFarland, 2018.

Chandra, Satish, *Medieval India: From Sultanat to the Mughals-Mughal Empire (1526–1748)*, Har Anand Publications, 2007.

Chandrababu, B.S., and L. Thilagavathi, *Woman, Her History and Her Struggle for Emancipation*, Bharathi Puthakalayam, 2009.

Chatterjee, Anjali, 'Role of Women in the Politics of Early Delhi Sultanate—A Case Study of Shah Turkan', *Proceedings of the Indian History Congress*, Vol. 59, 1998, pp. 404–06.

Chattopadhyaya, Kamaladevi, *Indian Women's Battle for Freedom*, Abhinav Publications, 1982.

Crawford, Elizabeth, *The Women's Suffrage Movement: A Reference Guide, 1866–1928*, Routledge, 1998.

Dalrymple, William, and Anita Anand, *Koh-i-noor: The Story of the World's Most Infamous Diamond*, Bloomsbury, 2017.

Daoud, Yousef, 'Daughter of Sufism: The Passion of Noor Inayat Khan', *Sufi: Journal of Mystical Philosophy and Practice*, 2010.

Dasgupta, Shahana, *Razia the People's Queen*, Rupa Publications, 2002.

Devi, D. Syamala, 'The Contribution of Women Parliamentarians in India', *The Indian Journal of Political Science*, Vol. 55, No. 4, 1994, pp. 411–16.

Dow, Alexander, *The History of Hindostan, Volume III*, T. Becket and P.A. De Hondt, London, 1772.

Elliot, Henry Miers, *History of India, in Nine Volumes—Vol. V, The Mohammedan Period as Described by Its Own Historians*, Jackson A.V. Williams (ed.), Cosimo Classics, 2008.

Elliot, Henry Miers, *The History of India, as Told by Its Own Historians: The Muhammadan Period; Volume 2*, John Dowson (ed.), Franklin Classics Trade Press, 2018.

Eraly, Abraham, *Emperors of the Peacock Throne: The Saga of the Great Mughals*, Penguin India, 2007.

Eraly, Abraham, *Last Spring: The Lives and Times of Great Mughals*, Penguin India, 2000.

Eraly, Abraham, *The Age of Wrath: A History of the Delhi Sultanate*, Viking, 2014.

Faruqui, Munis D., *The Princes of the Mughal Empire, 1504-1719*, Cambridge University Press, 2012.

Findly, Ellison Banks, *Nur Jahan: The Empress of India*, Oxford University Press, 1993.

Fletcher, Ian Christopher, Philippa Levine and Laura E. Nym Mayhall, *Women's Suffrage in the British Empire: Citizenship, Nation and Race*, Routledge, 2012.

Fortescue, Sir John, *A History of the British Army–Vol. III (1763–1793)*, Normanby Press, 2014.

Fox, Essie, 'The Maharajah, Duleep Singh ~ Queen Victoria's "Beautiful Boy"', *Rare Book Society of India*, 29 January 2019, https://tinyurl.com/mtxte8v2. Accessed on 3 June 2023.

Fuller, Jean Overton, *Double Webs*, Putnam, 1958.

Fuller, Jean Overton, *Noor-un-nisa Inayat Khan (Madeleine)*, East-West Publications Fonds, 1971.

Fuller, Jean Overton, *The Starr Affair*, V. Gollancz, 1954.

Gabbay, Alyssa, 'In Reality a Man: Sultan Iltutmish, His Daughter, Raziya, and Gender Ambiguity in Thirteenth Century Northern India', *Journal of Persianate Studies*, Vol. 4, No. 1, 2011, pp. 45–63.

Gandhi, Mohandas, and Amrit Kaur, *Letters to Rajkumari Amrit Kaur*, Navajivan Publishing House, 1961.

Garber, Megan, 'Night Witches: The Female Fighter Pilots of World War II', *The Atlantic*, 15 July 2013, https://tinyurl.com/p742h9d7.

Garodia Gupta, Archana, 'Didda, Controversial Queen of Kashmir', *Swarajya*, 26 April 2015, https://tinyurl.com/2p8wyk6n. Accessed on 23 June 2023.

Garodia Gupta, Archana, *The Women Who Ruled India: Leaders. Warriors. Icons.*, Hachette India, 2019.

Ghose, Anindita, and Parizaad Khan, 'Kitchen Archaeology', *mint*, 23 January 2010, https://tinyurl.com/mvjrcxp7. Accessed 4 June 2023.

Godden, Rumer, *Gulbadan: Portrait of a Rose Princess at the Mughal Court*, India Research Press, 2007.

Gott, Richard, *Britain's Empire: Resistance, Repression and Revolt*, Verso, 2012.

Greer, Margaret R., Walter D. Mignolo and Maureen Quilligan (eds), *Rereading the Black Legend: The Discourses of Religious and Racial Difference in the Renaissance Empires*, University of Chicago Press, 2008.

Grey, Edward (ed.), *The Travels of Pietro Della Valle in India: From the Old English Translation of 1664*, B. Franklin, 1892.

Guha, Ramachandra, *Gandhi: The Years that Changed the World*, Penguin Allen Lane, 2018.

Guha, Ramachandra, *India After Gandhi: The History of the World's Largest Democracy*, Picador, 2008.

Gupta, Subhadra Sen, *Mahal: Power and Pageantry in the Mughal Harem*, Hachette India, 2009.

Habibullah, A.B.M., 'Sul.t¯anah R¯aziah', *The Indian Historical Quarterly*, Vol. 16, No. 1, 1940.

Haeri, Shahla, *The Unforgettable Queens of Islam: Succession, Authority, Gender*, Cambridge University Press, 2020.

Helm, Sarah, *A Life in Secrets: Vera Atkins and the Missing Agents of WWII*, Anchor, 2007.

Hindi, Kanhaiya Lal, *Tareekh-e-Punjab*, 1875.

Honigberger, John Martin, *Thirty-Five Years in the East: Adventures, Discoveries, Experiments, and Historical Sketches, Relating to the Punjab and Cashmere; In Connection with Medicine, Botany, Pharmacy, Etc*, Bangabasi, 1852.

Husain, Mabdi, *The Rehla of Ibn Battuta*, Oriental Institute Baroda, 1976.

Hussain, Salma, *50 Great Recipes: Sharbats*, Roli & Janssen, 2005.

Iglikowski-Broad, Vicky, 'No Vote, No Census: The 1911 Suffrage Census Protests', *The National Archives*, 2 April 2020, https://tinyurl.com/3n6rasfd. Accessed on 4 June 2023.

Jagmohan, *My Frozen Turbulence in Kashmir*, Allied Publishers, 2014.

Jahan, Farhat, *Depiction of Women in the Sources of the Delhi Sultanate, (1206-1388)*, Centre of Advanced Study, Department of History, Aligarh Muslim University, 2012.

Jain, Simmi, *Encyclopaedia of Indian Women through the Ages: Period of Freedom Struggle*, Kalpaz Publications, 2003.

Jha, Shefali, 'Rights versus Representation: Defending Minority Interests in the Constituent Assembly', *Economic and Political Weekly*, Vol. 38, No. 16, 19 April 2003.

Juzjani, Minhaj-i Siraj, *Tabakat-i-Nasiri, Vol. I*, H.G. Raverty (trans.), Digital Library of India, 1881.

Kalaiselvi, L., 'Society, Religion and Culture in the Colonial Era; Contributions of the Rajahs of Sivaganga', *International Journal of Social Science and Economic Research*, Vol. 3, No. 11, November 2018.

Kalla, Krishnan Lal, *Eminent Personalities of Kashmir*, Discovery Publishing House, 1997.

Kang, Kanwarjit Singh, '"Sati" Choice before Maharaja Ranjit's Ranis', *The Tribune*, 27 June 2015, https://tinyurl.com/47mxjxbc. Accessed 3 June 2023.

Kaul, Ashish, *Didda: The Warrior Queen of Kashmir*, Rupa Publications, 2019.

Kaw, M.K., *Kashmir and Its People: Studies in the Evolution of Kashmiri Society*, APH Publishing, 2004.

Keay, John, *India: A History*, Harper Press, 2010.

Khan, Noor Inayat, *Twenty Jataka Tales*, East-West Publications Fonds, 1985.

Khan, Pir Vilayat Inayat, *Thinking Like the Universe: The Sufi Path of Awakening*, Thorsons, 2000.

Kramer, Rita, *Flames in the Field: The Story of Four SOE Agents in Occupied France*, CreateSpace Independent Publishing Platform, 2010.

Krishnan, Suhasini, 'The Humble Resting Place of Delhi's One & Only Queen', *Homegrown*, 8 June 2021, https://tinyurl.com/mr2ay448. Accessed on 5 June 2023.

Kudaisya, Gyanesh, and Tan Tai Yong, *The Aftermath of Partition in South Asia*, Routledge, 2002.

Kumar, Anu, 'How Akbar Came to Love Books though He Never Learnt to Read', *Scroll.in*, 7 November 2015, https://tinyurl.com/2yjrb3eu. Accessed on 4 June 2023.

Kumar, Madhan, *Thamizh Is Not Just a Language*, Educreation Publishing, 2017.

Kumar, Seshadri, 'India Should Be Grateful to Alauddin Khilji for Thwarting the Mongol Invasions', *The Wire*, 9 December 2017, https://tinyurl.com/4khvmaub.

Kurup, Pushpa, *Power Women: A Journey into Hindu Mythology, Folklore and History*, Bloomsbury India, 2018.

Lake, Robert J., *Routledge Handbook of Tennis: History, Culture and Politics*, Routledge, 2019.

Lakshmanjoo, Swami and John Hughes, *Light on Tantra in Kashmir Shaivism: Chapter One of Abhinavagupta's Tantraloka*, Universal Shaiva Fellowship, 2017.

Lal, Kishori Saran, *The Mughal Harem*, 1988.

Lal, Ruby, 'Historicizing the Harem: The Challenge of a Princess's Memoir', *Feminist Studies*, Vol. 30, No. 3, 2004.

Lal, Ruby, *Domesticity and Power in the Early Mughal World*, Cambridge University Press, 2005.

Lal, Ruby, *Empress: The Astonishing Reign of Nur Jahan*, Penguin Viking, 2018.

Law, Narendra Nath (ed.), *The Indian Historical Quarterly, Vol.16*, Caxton Publications, 1940.

Lownie, Andrew, *The Mountbattens: Their Lives & Loves*, BLINK Publishing, 2019.

Malik, Sonia, 'Restoration of Nur Jahan's Tomb to Begin Soon', *The Express Tribune*, 16 July 2012, https://tinyurl.com/5faydjfk. Accessed on 4 June 2023.

Manucci, Niccolo, and William Irvine, *Storia do Mogor: Or, Mogul India, 1653–1708*, Editions Indian, 1965.

Marcus, Leah, Janel Mueller, and Mary Beth Rose, *Elizabeth I: Collected Works*, University of Chicago Press, 2002.

Marks, Leo, *Between Silk and Cyanide: A Codemaker's War, 1941–1945*, Free Press, 2000.

Massey, Reginald, and Jamila Massey, *The Music of India*, Abhinav Publications, 1996.

Menon, Raja, 'Beastly End of a Beauty', *Outlook*, 5 February 2022, https://tinyurl.com/n72c748z. Accessed on 4 June 2023.

Migeon, Gaston, and Henri Saladin, *Art of Islam*, Parkstone International, 2012.

Mishra, Yogendra, *The Hindu Sahis of Afghanistan and the Punjab, A.D. 865–1026*, Vaishali Bhavan, 1972.

Monserrate, Antonio, *The Commentary of Father Monserrate, S.J. on His Journey to the Court of Akbar*, Asian Educational Services, 1922.

Moraes, Frank, *Jawaharlal Nehru*, Jaico Publishing House, 2007.

Mukherjee, Sumita, *Indian Suffragettes: Female Identities and Transnational Networks*, OUP India, 2018.

Mukhia, Harbans, *The Mughals of India*, Wiley India, 2008.

Mukhoty, Ira, *Daughters of the Sun: Empresses, Queens and Begums of the Mughal Empire*, Aleph Book Company, 2018.

Naravane, Susheila, *Acute Akbar Versus the Spirited Nur Jahan: The Soul's Journey Through Time and the Who's Who*, Troubador Publishing, 2018.

Nicoll, Fergus, *Shah-Jahan: The Rise and Fall of the Mughal Emperor*, Penguin India, 2018.

Pandit, B.N., *Essence of the Exact Reality or Paramarthasara of*

Abhinavagupta, Manoharlal Publishers, 1991.

Parr, Rosalind, *Citizens of Everywhere: Indian Nationalist Women and the Global Public Sphere, 1900–1952*, University of Edinburgh, 2018.

Parr, Rosalind, 'Solving World Problems: The Indian Women's Movement, Global Governance, and "The Crisis of Empire", 1933–46', *Journal of Global History*, Vol. 16, No. 1, March 2021.

Rabbani, G.M., *Ancient Kashmir*, Gulshan Publishers, 1981.

Rachel, Hannah, 'Noor Inayat, Indian-Origin Spy Who Could Feature on Britain's £50 Note', *The Week*, 23 October 2018, https://tinyurl.com/8732bkzy. Accessed on 4 June 2023.

Raina, Mohini Qasba, *Kashur: The Kashmiri Speaking People*, Trafford Publishing, 2013.

Raja, Siddharth, 'Tipu Sultan: The Forgotten Connection with India's First Sepoy Mutiny', *The Wire*, 10 November 2018, https://tinyurl.com/3nfanhah. Accessed on 23 June 2023.

Rajivlochan, M., 'The British Seeds of Secession', *Outlook*, 3 February 2018, https://tinyurl.com/mrya96tx. Accessed on 3 June 2023.

Rappaport, Helen, *Three Great Women: Encyclopedia of Women Social Reformers, Volume 1*, ABC-CLIO, 2001.

Report of the Health Survey and Development Committee Survey Vol. I, The Manager of Publications, Delhi, 1945.

Roychowdhury, Adrija, 'Explained: What Is the London Blue Plaque and Who Gets Feted by One?', *The Indian Express*, 30 August 2020, https://tinyurl.com/y4fmtzcb. Accessed on 4 June 2023.

Roychowdhury, Adrija, 'From Gouramma to Duleep Singh, the Tragic Lives of Queen Victoria's Many Colonial Godchildren', *The Indian Express*, 12 March 2021, https://tinyurl.com/

bddtcsd2. Accessed on 3 June 2023.

Rumi, Raza, *Delhi by Heart: Impressions of a Pakistani Traveller*, Harper, 2013.

Salam, Ziya Us, *Women in Masjid: A Quest for Justice*, Bloomsbury India, 2019.

Sen, Anikendra Nath, Devangshu Datta and Nilanjana S. Roy (eds), *Patriots, Poets and Prisoners: Selections from Ramananda Chatterjee's The Modern Review, 1907–1947*, HarperCollins, 2016.

Seyller, John William, Marika Sardar, and Audrey Truschke, *The Ramayana of Hamida Banu Begum, Queen Mother of Mughal India*, Museum of Islamic Art, 2020.

Sharma, Kumud, 'Power vs. Representation: Feminist Dilemmas, Ambivalent State and the Debate on Reservation for Women in India', Occasional Paper 28, Centre for Women's Development Studies, 1998.

Singh, Amarpal, *The Second Anglo-Sikh War*, Harper Collins, 2017.

Singh, Billy Arjan, *The Legend of the Maneater*, Sangam Books, 1993.

Singh, Khushwant, *Ranjit Singh: Maharaja of the Punjab*, Penguin Random House India, 2017.

Singh, Mohinder, *History and Culture of Panjab*, Atlantic Publishers and Distributors, New Delhi, 1989.

Sinha, Mrinalini, *Specters of Mother India: The Global Restructuring of an Empire*, Duke University Press, 2006.

Spragg, Iain, *London's Strangest Tales: Historic Royal Palaces*, Portico, 2014.

Srivastava, Gouri, *The Legend Makers: Some Eminent Muslim Women of India*, Concept Publishing, 2003.

Stein, M.A., *Kalhana's Rajatarangini: A Chronicle of the Kings of Kashmir*, Motilal Banarsidass, 2017.

Steinbach, Henry, *The Punjab Being a Brief Account of the Country of the Sikhs*, Sang-e-Meel Publications, 2005.

Tan, Tai Yong, and Gyanesh Kudaisya, *The Aftermath of Partition in South Asia: Routledge Studies in the Modern History of Asia*, Routledge, 2002.

Thackston, Wheeler McIntosh (trans.), *The Jahangirnama: Memoirs of Jahangir, Emperor of India*, Facsimile Publisher, 2016.

Ud Din, Mehraj, and Tawseef Mushtaq, 'Beyond Their Domestic Chores: Adventures of Women in the Politics of Kashmir Valley during Ancient Period', *Asian Journal of Science and Technology*, Vol. 8, No. 5, 2017.

Visram, Rozina, *Ayahs, Lascars and Princes: The Story of Indians in Britain 1700–1947*, Routledge, 2015.

Walthall, Anne, *Servants of the Dynasty–Palace Women in World History*, University of California Press, 2008.

Whitehead, Don, 'AP Was There: Allied Forces Liberate Paris from Nazis', *AP*, 25 August 2019, https://tinyurl.com/ycx4fjrw. Accessed on 3 June 2023.

www.ingramcontent.com/pod-product-compliance
Lightning Source LLC
LaVergne TN
LVHW100524110826
845146LV00002B/766